SPAIN

The **B**est of **S**panish   Interiors · Gardens · Architecture · Landscapes

SPAIN

The Best of Spanish · Interiors · Gardens · Architecture · Landscapes

Angus Mitchell

Photographs by Amparo Garrido

Edited by Tom Bell

A BULFINCH PRESS BOOK

Little, Brown and Company
Boston · Toronto · London

Endpapers Shimmering *azulejos* have remained a popular form of decoration since the Moors first introduced glazed tiles to Iberia over a thousand years ago.

Page 1 In Andalucia, entire palaces, such as the Casa de Pilato, have been wainscotted throughout with richly patterned tiles which help to cool the sweltering summer temperatures while adding another decorative dimension.

Pages 2 *and* 3 The remote emptiness of Extremadura. It was from here that the infamous Pizarro brothers deserted their occupations as swineherds and went in search of fortune to the New World where they set about conquering Peru.

DEDICATION

to **A. A**rce

Text copyright © 1990 by Angus Mitchell
Photographs copyright © 1990 by Amparo Garrido

Design by Rita Wüthrich

Map by Michael Hill

First United States Edition
First published in Great Britain by
George Weidenfeld and Nicolson Limited

ISBN 0-8212-1759-3
Library of Congress Catalog Card Number 90–55396
Library of Congress Cataloging-in-Publication information is available.

Bulfinch Press is an imprint and trademark of Little, Brown and Company (Inc.)
Published simultaneously in Canada by Little, Brown & Company (Canada) Limited

PRINTED IN ITALY

Pages 4 *and* 5 The whitewashed villages of the south, which hug the mountain-sides, are often thought to epitomise the Spanish landscape. But this is just one facet of its varied scenery.

CONTENTS

FOREWORD

My first sighting of Spain nearly 25 years ago was the road north along the coast out of Alicante. Its rape was already underway, a tawdry patchy drama at work along the dusty road which petered out from time to time to wind as a track through barren mounts in miniature. Now a motorway whisks you past the crimes of Benidorm or Calpe, but turn away from the sea and you really enter Spain.

Spain, the noisiest of countries, is characterized for me by a thousand keys of silence; the clockwork chorus of crickets, the strange acoustic of mountain air, lottery-ticket vendors, distant trains and aeroplanes, the sounds of creaking doors and the woodwind of bird song in my garden, an inevitable cockerel, goat bells, and everywhere the length and breadth of Spain, shouting in the streets.

My patch is the south. I first saw Granada under a thin dusting of snow. Now I've seen it in every weather and thought I knew every corner of the Alhambra. On each visit I am enchanted by the framed views this palace architecture affords, by the gentle work of devices repeated in rhythms that soothe and beguile, by the allusions to elegantly pruned woods, by cultivated waterways and the bold slow moving lines of light and shade. There is nothing new to say about this pleasure-dome, or its gardens; I leave that to the images of this book. But one caution first.

Left The Spanish patio garden is a combination of Islamic traditions and Roman design. Trickling fountains bear testimony to the importance of water in Islamic thought and the concept of paradise while the scale and architectural form are a reflection of the Roman atrium. Yet the patio has its own variations, each one developing over centuries in its own vacuum. So the patios of Córdoba are different from those of Seville or Granada.

Above A boldly decorated entrance to the cathedral of Charles V, which breaks out of the Islamic mosque of Córdoba.

I thought I knew every corner until, breathless in the heat one dusty afternoon, I discovered the cathedral underground that was this fortress's reservoir. The water is still there. You wind down perilous stairs through the cool damp air until the cavern opens out and it is a sort of miracle. But it is hard to repeat experiences in Spain; the reservoir, the Aljibe, is usually shut when I most need it.

Spain is rich with many faces, each with myriad disguises disfigured or enhanced by light and feeling. Our view from the farm across the plains of Granada, thirty miles of space spread out in front of the Sierra Nevada, is in a state of constant change. For half-an-hour a white village will light up, brilliant in the sun, and then slip back into the landscape, eclipsed by some other point. The mountains themselves can hide for weeks only to rise majestically, snow-capped, from their clouds to startle, intimidate or inspire.

I know no two travellers who seem to have found the same Spain, whether it is because an area has dominated their experience, or the echo of one civilization has them enthralled. Even if, like me, you do not presume to integrate with the Spaniards, finding it easier to move amongst them as an accepted, interested foreigner (when, I suppose, you should be less subject to the nuances of the regions), strange and powerful hauntings still work upon the mind. I cannot drive through those lonely Andalucian valleys without a sense of the narrow file of marching Catholic kings and their courts, Ferdinand and Isabella's crusades across Spain in the cold and wet of winter, or in the scorching heat. For me, Ronda, perched on its gorge, is the retreat of Romans. The bridge, like so many Roman remains, lives as a monument to their engineering like the lofty span over the Tagus at Alcántara or the aqueduct in Segovia. We are part of a long line of visitors – the French, Flemings, Germans and Italians all worked in Spain and left their mark. The English have a special role. In search of the exotic (magnified in fables) a steady stream of authors, artists and travellers have found a vivid dance of blood, music, bandits – and at small expense. Irving, Borrow, Byron, Ford, Disraeli, Hemingway and Brenan – to name a few – all broke ground in eulogizing their discoveries.

Romantic Spain is still there for those with the imagination and appetite, but I prefer the power of Spain's great natural beauty: the stitchwork of olive trees across the landscape, the extraordinary colours of the earth punctuated by man's work as builder and architect. It's never hard to find a mason in Spain; most agricultural workers know how to mix cement and use bricks. Their work is everywhere terracing the fields, part of the great tradition of building that is so important a movement today.

Not all images of Spain are as lyrical as those in this book. All travellers, even those leaving behind the raffia donkeys and garish blue-and-white china, know something of badly organized city traffic, brutal taxi-drivers, misshapen beggars with their tearing indignity. Caged birds, bleeding bulls, maimed dogs and broken horses exist, but so does the Spanish love of children.

One last word is a salute to the camera. These illustrations will either remind you of a beauty you know or will inspire you to find it for yourself. They catch an essence of history but belong, as undeniably as the open and close of the shutter, to one moment in the ever-changing kaleidoscope of Spain.

The Marchioness of Douro
Granada, 1990

Stone has offered endless possibilities for Spanish architects to explore their artistic imaginations, reinterpreting line and form in often highly sophisticated ways, as can be seen in this stone stairway.

INTRODUCTION

'Here,'

wrote Richard Ford,

nineteenth-century author of

A *Handbook for Travellers in Spain*,

'the voice of the Goth echoes amid Roman ruins,

and the step of the Christian treads on the heel of the Moor.'

Spain's historical identity has been shaped by a myriad external forces,

through which the country has found

its soul.

As a country, Spain cannot be summed up in broad general statements. It is a nation composed of different languages, customs, attitudes, histories, people and climates; where nothing is simply *Spanish*. Yet Hispanic life, as perceived not only in Europe but also in parts of Latin America, has a recognizable character all its own, a powerful force in the shaping of the modern world. Even today, in the more isolated areas of the country, there survives a way of life which appears strangely out of touch with the twentieth century; and if a generalization must be made then Spain should be considered a land of finely balanced extremes.

From the discovery of a New World in 1492 to the final loss of most of its colonies at the end of the nineteenth century, the term 'Spain' has meant Castile, the great wide tableland at the centre of the country. It was *castellano* which became the language of colonization, and from Castile the empire was ruled, an empire which, after the addition of the Portuguese colonies under Philip II in 1580, included all Iberia, the south of Italy and Lombardy, Holland and Belgium, parts of eastern France, Central and South America, most of southern and south-western North America, the Philippines, Madeira, the Azores and Cape Verde Islands, Guinea, Congo, Angola, Ceylon, Borneo, Sumatra, the Moluccas and many other settlements on the Asiatic seaboard.

Cultural influences have entered Spain from every corner of the globe. During the sixteenth and seventeenth centuries, when galleons of gold returned on the spring tides to the Atlantic ports of Cadiz, Huelva and Seville, Spain enjoyed its imperial splendour. The building of extravagant noble palaces, the lavish interior embellishment of churches and cathedrals, the cultivation of courtly magnificence and patronage of the arts were carried out on a level of extravagance to which later European royal households could only aspire. The Habsburg kings who ruled from 1517 to 1700 were strongly affected by their Flemish origins and Spain developed a deeper north European character expressed through its painting and architecture.

Great reserves of gold, gained from the mining of precious metals in Aztec and Inca lands, were spent on the maintenance of the first European worldwide empire, a formidable and ultimately impossible task. As a result, the people and lands of Castile were gradually exhausted by the burden of an empire too large to be effectively controlled.

In 1700 the Habsburg line ended with the death of Charles II the Impotent. Flemish taste bowed to that of the French with the accession of the Bourbons

through Philip of Anjou, who had been brought up at the court at Versailles. French influence on Spain was not new. It had a parallel in the great monastic movements of the eleventh and twelfth centuries, which had introduced Romanesque and Gothic architecture along the pilgrim road to Santiago. The medieval kingdoms of Navarre and Catalonia had stretched into southern France, while Basque culture extends to this day across the Pyrenees.

Trade with the colonies improved throughout the eighteenth century, and during the long enlightened reign of Charles III (1759–88), far-reaching economic and religious reforms created the conditions of modern Spain. Charles had also been King of Naples and Sicily, and as a child had witnessed the excavations at Herculaneum and Pompeii. They had inspired him to establish botanical gardens and a museum of natural sciences, and to inaugurate a Neo-classical revival.

The link between Naples and the peninsula was another vital force in the formation of the Spanish heritage. The Borgia family, which played such an important part in Italian history during the sixteenth century, emigrated from Valencia to Rome. During the Renaissance there was a strong link between the two countries which flourished during the late

seventeenth century with the arrival of the Baroque age, which originated in Rome.

The invasion of the armies of Napoleon in 1808 in effect marked the start of a long, dark decline for Spain. The American colonies revolted; Spain was domestically too fragile to resist. The *desamortización* or dissolution of the monasteries in the 1830s broke up the landed power of the church. The monarchy, successively overawed, extinguished and restored by army commanders, was equally ill-served by frequent coalition governments. Revolts followed assassinations and government breakdowns. Differences of political ideology splintered cities, villages and families. By the end of the century the war with America, sparked off by a revolt in Cuba, and the consequent destruction of the Spanish fleet in 1898 marked the end of Spain as a colonial power.

The beginning of the new century was marked by the brilliant and artistic 'Generation of 1898', which took its name from the date of Spain's massive naval defeat, and the brief flowering of Modernism. The movement was largely inspired by a revival of Catalan nationalism. Intellectuals and scholars reinterpreted Spain's past in the context of its current political humiliation, but they did not manage to halt the progress of Spain's deep-seated destructive

tendencies, and events reached a nihilistic finale in the Civil War (1936–39) which was followed by a long period of European isolation.

Many placed the blame on the failure of centralized government to recognize strong regional differences. The struggle of local loyalties against the spirit of national unity is a recurring theme throughout Spanish history. As one commentator put it, the various regions were like a collection of small bodies tied together by a rope of sand.

A succession of foreign invasions together with a flourishing trade throughout the Mediterranean helped to reinforce Spain's regional differences. The primitive Neolithic tribes who migrated north from the southern Sahara and settled the coastal plains and central river basins of Spain were strong independent people. Gradually they absorbed the currents of oriental influence which now permeated the Mediterranean. In the earliest Greek histories they were called Iberians. It is known that the Phoenicians traded with an Iberian kingdom called Tartessos, a civilization which has never been located precisely but which existed somewhere along the Quadalquivir basin of Andalucia. The Tartessians grew rich from mining the deposits of silver, copper and lead in the hilly uplands of the Rio Tinto. In exchange they received carved ivory, alabaster vessels, jewellery and ceramics. Later, waves of Greeks and Carthaginians were to found new cities all along the coast. While the Iberian culture of the south and east flourished under the influence of colonizers from the eastern Mediterranean, the rest of the country witnessed the gradual and peaceful penetration of the peninsula by Celts through the Pyrenees and central Europe. Slowly these external cultures were absorbed by the Iberian and Celtic tribes of the interior. The enthroned priestesses, hewn from vast slabs of limestone, the granite bulls and undeciphered languages are the few remnants of this indigenous people. They speak of a high level of eastern acculturation.

All this was overlaid by the expansion of Rome through the Mediterranean world. By the last century BC, the peninsula was completely Romanized: roads and bridges opened up the interior allowing all three provinces – Tarraconensis, Lusitania and Baetica – to flourish. Many cities and roads in modern Spain are built upon Roman foundations. In fact, both Trajan and Hadrian, two of Rome's greatest emperors, were natives of Iberia.

By the sixth century AD northern influences had briefly replaced those of south and east. Peoples from eastern and central Europe settled different areas of the peninsula: Swabians in Galicia; Alans in the Pais Vasco; and Visigoths, who picked up the weak reins of government in the central Meseta and established their capital at Toledo. For three centuries they maintained a loose supremacy that collapsed with minimal resistance in 711, when the Arab lieutenant Tarik crossed the Straits of Gibraltar from Morocco. Within three years he brought the whole of Iberia into the fold of Islam. Only a small Christian enclave remained in the isolated mountains of the north.

Al-Andalus was the name the Arabs gave to their new kingdom, a land they considered to be the fifth earthly paradise. They ruled in the south for seven centuries, and philosophers, poets, mystics, translators and scientists flourished under their ruler's benevolent protection. The introduction of Islamic culture, so prolific in both art and literature, had an indelible effect on Spain. But most of all the regime was tolerant, allowing Moslems, Christians and Jews to live in harmonious co-existence. The cross-fertilization of artistic understanding that ensued produced such decorative styles as Mozarabic and Mudéjar, unique to the civilization of Spain.

The first dynasty, the Umayyads, established their caliphate at Córdoba and produced a line of outstanding and often brilliant rulers. By the tenth century Córdoba had become the fulcrum of Moslem and Christian intellectual life in Spain, and the most enlightened city in Europe. The great mosque and the city-palace of Medina az-Zahra mark the zenith of this artistic flowering. Luxuriant interiors and exotic gardens gave expression to Islamic belief. Vast, barren stretches of land were opened up to cultivation through the ingenious methods of Moorish irrigation.

With the fall of the Umayyads, the country was broken up into *taifas*, or petty kingdoms, that resembled the medieval Italian city-states; and sultan vied with sultan to acquire the most prestigious library, or to attract the most learned poets and men of science to their courts.

In the eleventh and twelfth centuries waves of fanatic Moorish tribes, the Almoravids and Almohads, crossed the Atlas mountains into Spain in an attempt to maintain a unified Islamic front against the gradual Christian advance, but conquest and civilization led to decadence and defeat as Moslem Spain faded inexorably away.

At the same time a new Spain was slowly forming in the north, where the aggressively Christian and military ideals of the *reconquista* inspired the gradual reoccupation of Moslem territory. The newly reconquered centre and south were defended by a network of fortified *castillos*, some of them held by the military orders – the knights of Santiago and Alcantara, and the Templars – who were afforded a regular supply of foreign crusaders by the pilgrimage route to Santiago.

Masons, master builders, glaziers and other craftsmen arrived from all parts of Europe to help in the construction of this new frontier of Christendom. By the eleventh century the kingdoms of León, Castile, Navarre and Aragón formed a defensive block along the course of the river Duero. In 1212 the Battle of Las Navas de Tolosa saw the balance of power shift conclusively away from the Moslems to the Christians. There now began a period of Christian urban development and the establishment of two universities, one at Palencia in 1212 and the other at Salamanca in 1254.

As important as the gradual success of the offensive against Islam was the unification of Catalonia, ruled by the Counts of Barcelona, with the kingdom of Aragón. The Catalan-Aragónese seaborne empire stretched from southern France and the Balearic Islands to Sicily. In the fifteenth century, the alliance of the kingdoms of Castile and Aragón was sealed by the marriage of Isabella of Castile and Fernando II of Aragón, which led to the nation's unification.

On 1 January 1492 the last Moorish enclave, Granada, was finally captured, and on Christmas Day of the same year Columbus discovered America. Spain, in the space of a few months, had grown from a frontier society into a worldwide empire.

The long crusade against Islam and the opening up of the Americas are the two fundamental events responsible for forging Spain's historical identity. But Flemish, French and Italian influences, introduced by monastic houses, ruling dynasties and trade relations, are no less important especially in terms of their artistic significance. The seven hundred years of Moorish occupation is a subject which often falls prey to romantic exaggeration. Islamic culture in a European setting is strange and exotic, and many influences have lingered on into the present. There is no doubt it was an exceptional civilization, and through the long years of reconquest Spain found its soul. But Islam is only a part of Spain's cultural heritage, just as the harsh dry Meseta is only one aspect of its diverse landscape.

Civilizations can be perceived on many levels. Using the broad themes of Elements, Details, Interiors, Gardens and finally Modernism, this book attempts to define the particular quality of life in Spain.

Left Monumental city walls dating as far back as the eleventh century can be found throughout Spain, the battlements – often made with Roman foundation stones – signifying a turbulent history.

11

Above The bull has become a symbol of Spain and its presence can be seen everywhere – from bronze fountain heads gushing forth cooling waters to the finely wrought *aldabas*, or iron rings, that decorate Spanish doors to the spectacle of the bullring itself.

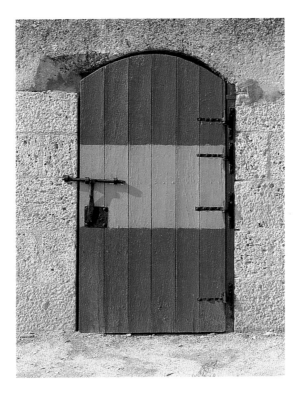

ELEMENTS

Spain

is a land of contrasts.

The central tableland, where the light dazzles

and horizons seem boundless, is the antithesis of the north,

with its verdant fields and gentle contours,

or the south, with its olive groves

and whitewashed

villages.

Landscape

On a map of the world, the outline of Iberia at the south-western extremity of Europe looks quite neat. But this is deceptive. For the shape of the peninsula, often likened to a piece of bullhide pegged out in the sun to dry, gives little indication of the stunning contrasts of the interior.

Spain has the character of a small continent broken up into sharply diverse landscapes. The country is a constant alchemy of mountains and dusty steppes, dry barely-arable expanses and splashes of rich fertility. From the forests and wetlands of the north to the unbounded olive groves of the south flash images of African savannah, South American pampas, even the beaches of Australia. These myriad variations are responsible for some of Europe's most enigmatic ecological secrets.

Without understanding something of the rich, sculptural complexity of the landscape it would be impossible to grasp the subtleties which divide the habits and customs of the people. Atlantic and Saharan weather systems break above Iberia causing extraordinary seasonal extremes. Winter storms can be so torrential as to eclipse the light; while in August, millions of sun-worshippers from northern Europe descend each week to soak up the ultra-violet rays.

Yet the range of both climate and altitude lend such scope to the land that almost anything can be grown; in fact, most indigenous species of European fruit and vegetable have at some time adapted to the conditions. In the last few decades modern market gardening methods have also seen the successful introduction of kiwi fruit farms in Galicia and mango and avocado plantations in the 'tropical' valleys of Andalucia. Elsewhere large stretches of previously sterile land have been irrigated and covered with makeshift plastic greenhouses. They supply the continent with summer vegetables through the winter. It is often forgotten that the vineyards of La Mancha produce more litres of table wine than any other single cooperative in the world and that huge surpluses of Castilian wheat are exported to the Soviet Union.

In spring when the first of the winter snows start to thaw, the rivers fill, light showers veil the land, the country is blanketed with lush colour and the air scented with herbal aromas. To follow the progress of spring, which enters from the south with the migrating birds in February and turns into summertime four months later in the fresh Galician May, is to witness an extraordinary symphony of sound,

Left Galicia in the north-west of Spain, with its fertile valleys and rolling hills, is often likened to Ireland or Brittany. Rural isolation has preserved a strong sense of regional culture.

Right and below The thatched dwellings of Cabreiro on the Galician border have supplied sanctuary to pilgrims for centuries. The same building materials are used for the granaries in which maize and grain are stored.

Below right Spain has over 2,000 miles of quiet secluded bays that face onto both the Atlantic and the Mediterranean. The country's links with the sea are of historic importance, dating back to the sixteenth century when Spain was the head of a maritime empire and galleons of gold returned on the spring tides to the port of Cadiz.

15

16

A great part of the central Meseta is composed of Cretaceous and Jurassic limestone, which in some areas has eroded into spectacular landforms such as defiles and deep gorges.

North of Cuenca lies the Ciudad Encantada, the enchanted city, where the most haunting examples of karstic erosion are found. Vast billowing shapes connected by natural tunnels and bridges create the sense of an abandoned city locked in the surreal imagination.

movement and colour.

In contrast to this are the empty expanses of the Meseta, burnt brown by the relentless heat of summer. This is a time when dust blows in circles above the thin earth of Aragón; when the interminable arid horizons of the Upper Duero tableland grow stiff with wheat; when the dunes of Almería, where so many spaghetti-westerns were shot, resemble the frontier of Arizona and Mexico; when the stillness is broken by nothing save the shimmering currents of heat haze, and shy geckoes darting between shadows and flies; when the land and sky seem to merge inextricably into a watery horizon, thinly broken by the silhouette of distant sierras.

Every region without exception has its mountains or sierras, speckled with semi-deserted, semi-ruinous villages where people and animals still live under the same roof. In these rustic pockets, nature has been harnessed to fit the needs of the inhabitants enabling each community to exist in a virtual state of agrarian self-sufficiency.

Mountains have been both the scourge and saviour of the Spanish, hindering communication and checking any even national development. In fact, the separatism of most Spanish regions can to a large extent be explained geographically. At the same time, they have supplied cities with water, generated enough electricity to make the country one of the major industrial nations of the world and released rich mineral deposits of iron ore, silver, gold, mercury, uranium, oil and coal.

The Pyrenees were long considered the great barrier to European integration, a cause of insularity and a physical and psychological frontier. This is perhaps, where Africa begins. In these days of jet travel, the ominous character of the range is often forgotten. Its jagged peaks rise like a gigantic portcullis traversed by a handful of narrow, twisting passes often blocked by snow and glaciers for days on end. Yet the secluded glens remain a refuge for several endangered species of birds and insects which thrive among the pine forests and meadows. The mountains are drained by a labyrinth of valleys which carve their way southwards through Catalonia, Aragón, Navarre and Euskadi. This is a land of stone-built villages where life remains as constant as the crystal-clear rivers which rush blindly towards the Ebro basin.

From the western extremity of the Pyrenees rises the other great northern massif, the Cordillera Cantábrica. Like a great yoke of muscle it thrusts from east to west, from the Basque lands all the way to Portugal. These are wild, verdant, pluviose moun-

17

Above The silence that hangs over the undulating limestone sierras of the south is disturbed ony by the clear echo of distant goat bells. The land is too dry to support anything other than sparse patches of scrub and wild herbs. Many of the small farm holdings which once eked a living from the hard earth have long since been deserted.

Left Deep limestone gorges criss-cross the Meseta creating natural barriers which have land-locked many villages for centuries, helping to preserve an almost medieval way of life.

Preceding pages Early morning mists rise above the sierras of Castile, revealing golden swathes of cut reeds, or *mimbre*, spread out across the land to dry in the heat of the sun.

Right and below Since its introduction by the Romans, the olive has remained the staple crop of Spanish agriculture in all regions except those bordering the Atlantic. Thousands of acres throughout Andalucia, Castile and the Balearic Islands are planted with groves of grey-green olive trees which thrive in the arid, unwatered earth.

20

Right The castellated horizon of Trujillo rises above the remote emptiness of Extremadura. It was from here that the infamous Pizarro brothers deserted their occupations as swineherds and went in search of fortune to the New World.

Far right Small villages, tucked away in remote sierras, have survived the ages of Arab, Christian and bandit rule to become as intrinsic to the Spanish landscape as the sun.

During the fifteenth century the Castilian economy was founded upon the prosperous wool trade with Flanders. The annual migration of millions of sheep along the *cañadas*, which run from the winter pastures of the south to the summer grazing lands of the north, is a tradition which has been maintained to the present day.

Cuenca was a prosperous agricultural market town which undoubtedly benefited from the wool trade. The original settlement was founded on a promontory, surrounded by the rivers Jucar and Huécar, which formed a natural fortress. Many of the houses hang precariously over the cliff side.

tains where cattle wander freely along the high roads, and villages with their rust-coloured rooftops lie sleepily in the steep wooded valleys.

The regions of Cantabria and Asturias embrace the heart of the range. The mountains sweep down along the Costa Verde in a spectacular series of cliffs, quiet bays and spry fishing villages. Out of this land, made green and luxuriant with rain, surge the Picos de Europa, the most magnificent of all the Cordilleran peaks. Here hay meadows supply secluded tranquillity for butterflies and orchids which breed in profusion, and small farmhouses lie hidden away between the steep, rocky gorges and passes.

Throughout the north of Spain the imagery of pilgrimage is so strong as to be hauntingly inseparable from the landscape. Since the ninth century, pilgrims have been making the journey to Compostela and the shrine of St James, and all along the road stand the great monuments of the cult. Several paths converge at Puente de la Reina, the bridge that rises graciously from the woodlands of Navarre. From there pilgrims follow the 'cultural highway', marked by the symbol of the cockle shell. On the way they pass by the vineyards of La Rioja, where many of the country's greatest wines are matured in old oaken vats, before entering Castile itself. The

23

Right The picturesque village of Albarracín still preserves nine of the square towers that mark its eleventh-century wall, constructed at a time when southern Aragón formed part of the strategic frontier with the Moorish kingdom of Al-Andalus.

Below The Sierra de Guadarrama, part of the central massif cutting across Castile, is covered in snow for much of the winter. The waters which run off the slopes supply Madrid with much of its water. On the west side of the sierra, a stream feeds the large reservoir above the Bourbon palace of La Granja where the vast Baroque fountains consume as much water as an entire town.

path then wends its way through the quiet, open plain between the great cathedral cities of Burgos and León, and across the desolate border to Galicia. Here nature makes its mark on every granite building in luminous patches of brightly coloured lichen and moss, which breed profusely in the clean, moist air. The journey finally ends at the cathedral of Santiago de Compostela, the most sacred site in Christendom after St Peter's in Rome and the holy city of Jerusalem.

Galicia, 'land of cider and lobsters', has a mournful, melancholic and windswept air. Its people are closely connected to the forces of the ocean, their culture steeped in Celtic myth. Streams race between hills planted with apple orchards and the vineyards that produce the fresh local wine, a perfect accompaniment to a dozen oysters. The pastureland is often compared to Ireland, a green country of glades and chestnut trees waiting for the next shower of rain.

The Galician coastline is a jagged succession of rias, deep winding estuaries dotted with fishing hamlets. At the far western edge, on the Costa de Muerte or 'Coast of Death', lies Cape Finisterre, the ancient end of the world until Columbus proved otherwise. 'A fearful place,' as George Borrow de-

24

26

Gerona in Catalonia was one of the leading cities of the Aragónese-Catalan empire. The houses along the waterfront form a colourful façade behind which lies one of the most perfectly restored Jewish quarters in Europe, with its maze of steep cobbled streets.

scribed it, 'in seasons of wind and tempest, when the long swell of the Atlantic pouring in, is broken into surf and foam by the sunken rocks with which it abounds. Even in the calmest day there is a rumbling and a hollow roar in that bay which fills the heart with uneasy sensations' (*The Bible in Spain*, first published in 1845).

Rising from the south of the Atlantic seaboard and the barrier of these wild, virescent mountains spreads the huge central tableland, the Meseta, covering almost half of the entire surface area of the country. Across these empty reaches the great legends of Spain were formed: over the lands of Old Castile, Rodrigo Diaz, alias El Cid, Spain's greatest national hero, waged his adventurous life as an eleventh-century soldier of fortune. The uninhabited expanses where he rode are still burnished with the same heat of summer and biting winter wind while the sky remains perpetually blue.

In the remote southern stretches of Castile the knight-errant, Don Quixote, set out in search of his chivalric fantasy unable to distinguish reality from illusion. Though the silhouettes of a few windmills still decorate the horizon, the land has become an interminable, undulating, monotonous expanse of wheat, vines and olive groves, occasionally punctuated with an anonymous farm village.

Castile was the force behind the rise of the sixteenth-century empire. A thriving wool trade turned the Meseta towns into the business centres of Europe, and Castilians grew rich from the transhumant flocks of merino sheep which were driven each year along the *cañadas*, or migration paths, between their seasonal pastures, a tradition which continues to this day.

The area is now sadly depopulated: mighty *castillos* lie in ruins; once proud villages have been ostracized by time. Only the jaded magnificence of cities like Toledo, Avila, Segovia, Burgos and Salamanca, raising their great cathedral spires above the plain, remind the traveller of the old Castilian hegemony. Even their populations are a shadow of former days, and only Madrid has maintained its position as an administrative centre and capital of the nation.

Philip II chose Madrid as the permanent home of the Spanish court in 1561 for no better reason than its site, which was at the centre of the peninsula and close to good hunting grounds. It has always been an artificial capital, landlocked and without any significant river; but these topographical drawbacks have not prevented it becoming the largest city in the land. From the gardens of the royal palace it is possible to look out across the sprawling cityscape

27

R*ight and far right* Córdoba stands on the river Guadalquivir at the centre of a rich farming district at the foot of the sierras. The Guadalquivir was the principal artery of Granada and was navigable as far as Córdoba, which gave the city its strategic importance. The most stimulating city in the west from 756 to 1010, Córdoba produced a line of brilliant astrologers, poets, doctors and mathematicians. Islam was the catalyst for these thinkers, and the city became a centre of Islamic pilgrimage in the west – at its height Córdoba had a population of over 300,000 people and over 300 mosques. In the surrounding streets, a medieval atmosphere is preserved in the narrow lanes, crooked little plazas and patios glimpsed through iron gates.

to the Sierra de Guadarrama, part of the great central massif slicing Castile along a south-west axis. These desolate mountains have long been the refuge of displaced communities who found sanctuary here during times of persecution. The irregular highlands run out into Portugal as waves of barren rocky heights which at times look hauntingly volcanic. The villages of these sierras continue a way of life which has survived for centuries – and the acres of terraced land encircling each *pueblo* are still worked with mules and horses. Almond and cherry trees thrive in the dry, sunny climate and from late January to April the landscape shimmers with spring blossom and the air drones with the sound of honey bees.

These thriving hill-villages decrease in number as the land descends southwards into Extremadura, the ancient kingdom 'beyond the Duero'. And 'extreme' indeed is its people's way of life, wrought with much labour from the baked, acidic earth. The great birds of prey, circling endlessly in a steel-blue sky and scanning the *dehesa* for vermin, echo the unceasing cycle of human conflict in this frontier region between Castile and Portugal.

Nevertheless, Extremadura's internal antagonisms have been its saviour. The habitat retains one of the most unadulterated ecosystems left in Europe. The cork and holm oak forests in the Monfragüe National Park serve as eyries for some of the last breeding pairs of black storks, imperial eagles, black vultures and many other predatory birds which thrive in the bare escarpment between the river Tagus and the river Guadiana.

Extremadura was also the homeland of a large number of conquistadors who laid waste the ancient civilizations of South America. Deserting their livelihoods as herdsmen, each man ventured forth in search of his own El Dorado, discovering instead Mexico, Peru, the Amazon, the Mississippi and the Pacific. Some returned to heap honour upon their families, building vast Renaissance palaces in towns like Cáceres and Trujillo, which tower like stone oases above the hypnotic wilderness.

For many of these men the route to the New World began aboard a caravel setting out from Seville. Before reaching the Atlantic they had to navigate the Guadalquivir, the 'big river', the artery of Andalucia. Their last memories of the Spanish peninsula before venturing into the unknown must have been the olive groves, fruit orchards, vineyards, and forests of pine and mastic trees growing in the golden-

29

ochre earth and set against the distant outline of the southern sierras.

While much of the coast of Andalucia has been corrupted by twentieth-century development, vast stretches of the interior have resisted the temptations of progress and remain much as they were five hundred, a thousand, two thousand years ago. The vines and olive groves introduced by the Romans and the oranges and lemons first planted by the Moors are now as characteristic of the landscape by day as the brightly defined stars of the Andalucian night.

Andalucia, where life is perpetually exaggerated by the colour, the *alegría* and the heat, never ceases to grip the imagination of travellers: the villages of the Alpujarras, plastered like swallows' nests against the mountain sides; the annual pilgrimage to El Rocío, traversing the surreal wetlands of the

Doñana National Park; and the flamingoes nesting on the salt lake of Fuente de Piedra make it a land of blazing contrasts and inimitable natural beauty.

In a similar way, each of the Balearic Islands is a variation on the landscape themes of the southern Levantine mainland. Mallorca, Formentera and Ibiza are at once lush, arid, mountainous and flat, but they all possess magnificent sea views comparable to any in the Mediterranean. Menorca, the most northern island of the archipelago, billows with soft green hills studded with mysterious Bronze Age *talayots*, possibly the earliest dwellings established in Europe.

In an age when the landscape of so many countries appears domesticated and contrived by constant human interference, the lasting attraction of Spain is the dominance of the wild and the continued harmony of man with nature.

30

L*eft* Bell towers and orange-tiled roof tops, broken up by patches of white walls and the ascendant trunks of cypress trees, characterise the southern rural townscapes.

F*ar left* Cork oak and ilex forests cover large areas of the south. In their midst fighting bulls once roamed free; eagles still circle above in the passive air currents, scanning the *dehesa* for prey. Today, Spain exports great quantities of cork to the vineyards of France.

Colour

Colours are almost a universe unto themselves, everywhere dissolving and re-forming under the effects of the light, the seasons and the landscape. They are a natural symbol for all people, emotive of tradition, of personality, of mood; a link between nature and the human spirit. In their reflection of the outer world upon the inner consciousness, colours are a constantly changing medium of self-expression.

Anyone who has been to a fiesta will understand the role of colour in the life of Spaniards. No one can help but be intoxicated by the vibrant, exuberant parade at fiesta time: the señoritas frocked out in an exhilarating blend of flamenco and rustic costumery, bedazzling polka-dot gowns and colourful shawls; *jinetes* riding upon perfectly groomed horses with their richly embroidered saddlery; children dressed with equal extravagance, excitedly waiting for the procession to begin.

As carriages emblazoned with lilies and carnations start to move, and the strident noise of the band begins to rise above the chatter, the street swims in a tumultuous cacophony. Later, under the mantle of darkness, fireworks will explode like crystal rainbows over the heads of the revellers. Colour is momentarily exalted to the level of ritualistic celebration.

Francisco Goya was one of many artists who tried to capture the strong, animated colours of everyday life in Spain. His early paintings resonate with the dazzling light of the land, heightened with white lead; the delicate blues of the Castilian sky; golden expanses filled with bucolic laughter and merrymaking. These bright, almost manic, interpretations of pastoral joy sit uncomfortably beside the grisaille panels of his dark last years depicting the phantasmagoric horror of his imagination.

Nearly all Spanish painters have been fascinated by the contrast of light and shade, the half tones, dark accents, the reflections and highlights of their homeland. The shadows of the great portraits of Zurbarán grow ever darker with age in sharp tonal contrast to his splashes of almost visionary brightness. This is a recurring impression in Spanish painting.

Living contrasts stare at travellers from every southern village. The dazzling luminosity of the limewashed walls becomes whiter with each fresh coat of calcimine, presenting a startling backdrop for the widows who shuffle through the streets going about their daily chores, dressed in black

32

Left Painted façades, shuttered windows and wrought-iron balconies are a familiar sight throughout Spain.

Right Few cities in the world can match the vibrant colour of Seville, most outrageously exploited during the weeks of the Fería Abril, or April Fair.

Below Strong afternoon shadows fall across a typical balcony in Andalucia; locally woven *esparto* matting has been placed over the window to keep the high temperatures out and let any breezes in.

Below right Bustling markets full of fruit and vegetable stalls proudly display produce brought in from all over the country. The climate of Spain is so varied almost anything can be grown.

Left Earthy colours of terracotta and ochre are widely used for exterior walls in the central regions of the country.

Above Traditional copper vessels are displayed on a kitchen shelf for the aesthetic quality of their colour, rather than any functional purpose.

A*bove* The tonal graduation of stone ranges from the golden hues of Salamanca and the deep red of Aragón to the grey granite of Castile and Galicia, and the sandstone of Andalucia which under certain lights turns pale pink in colour.

R*ight* Ochroid colours, both inside and out, have a long-standing popularity with the Spanish. Here, a simple arched doorway is brought to life by the yellow calcimined wall behind. The earliest use of specifically Spanish colours can be traced back to Mozarabic manuscripts produced in the monasteries of the north during the ninth and tenth centuries, in which deep vegetable hues of red and yellow were first co-ordinated.

from head to foot. In the bright days of summer, colours radiate with a depth and intensity which seem to burn the muscles of the eye. In the bullring, the seats in the *sombra* are twice as expensive as those in the *sol*.

The quest for colour in Spain began with the Phoenicians, who dived for the murex snail off the Mediterranean coast and boiled the shells to extract the purple dye. Later Hispano-Roman mosaics show the use of sophisticated shades of blue, yellow and red which were such popular colours for interior decoration. Even more imposing are the early illuminated manuscripts of the Asturians, especially the eighth-century *Beatus de Liébana*, a vividly illustrated commentary upon the apocalypse. Each page is minutely detailed with strong vegetable hues of scarlet, crimson, yellow, wine red and verdigris, which shine with the same intensity after a thousand years of exposure.

The Arabs first developed a philosophy of colour based upon earlier Greek theory. Each string of the lute was dyed and matched with one of the four divisions of the body. Red corresponded to joy (blood), black to melancholy (black bile), yellow to anger (yellow bile) and white to fear (mucous). Physical equilibrium was dependent upon the balance of these four elements; Moslem physicians sometimes used music to cure the psychic disorders of their patients and the art of flamenco descends directly from these Hispano-Arab ideas.

By contrast, Christian use of colour was motivated by concrete and practical reasons. Colour combinations were used extensively for the recognition of clans and kindreds on the battlefield. Heraldic colours indicated particular loyalties and status. This is well illustrated by the traditional story surrounding the origins of the flag of Catalonia. During the successful capture of Paris from the Normans in 886, great bravery was displayed by one of the Counts of Barcelona, Wilfred the Hairy. His exploits were acknowledged by the Frankish king, Charles the Bald, who dipped his fingers in the wounds of his ally and ran them across his shield, engraving for evermore four crimson bars upon the Catalan escutcheon.

As important as the painting of ensigns was the polychrome decoration of religious reliquaries and altarpieces (*retablos*). The practice graduated from the use of subtle vegetable tones on Romanesque and Gothic statuettes and grew into a gilded extravagance during the years of Renaissance and Baroque prosperity. In the seventeenth century every diocese appointed a 'Pintor de Imaginería' to

A view across the Beach of Shells to the island of Santa Clara, which rises from the bay of San Sebastián. The most cosmopolitan city of Spain, San Sebastián became the preferred royal summer residence during the nineteenth century and continues to attract people in search of a magnificent location, mild climate, clear blue waters and the best of Basque cooking.

15

Bright colours both accentuate and absorb the dazzling light, often creating stunning tonal combinations. Pale yellow walls act as a sunny backdrop to the vivid colours of a tiled bench; doorways reflect the blue of the wide Castilian sky or the jade green of Islam, the sacred colour of the oasis. But, in the end, those colours taken directly from nature are most character-istic of Spain.

put the finishing touches to pictures, altars and furnishings; the combination of gold and red spread like fire throughout the interiors of Spanish churches.

If you ask a Spaniard what is the most important colour of the nation, the answer will usually be red. Red is the colour of passion, beauty and religion. The scarlet carnation is the national flower. The name 'Alhambra' translates from the Arabic for 'The Red'. Even the Hall of Bisons, in the prehistoric cave of Altamira in the mountains of Cantabria, is remarkable for the deep earthy tints used to fill the fine charcoal outlines of these exceptionally vivid figurations painted over twelve thousand years ago. Red is embedded in the Hispanic psyche.

But even as the colour red signifies life and passion, it equally signifies death. From the moment the picador first shoots his lance into the glistening back of the bull causing blots of dark red blood to spread across the burnt-ivory skin, until the dead beast is finally dragged by mules and chains from the arena, leaving its stain of crimson sand, the vision of blood is a vision of sacrifice and death.

Blue has more sedate qualities. It is the colour of the wide Castilian sky, and of the seas which wash against Iberia's east and west coasts. It is the colour in which so much popular coastal architecture is painted: stark blue against ebullient white transforms Mediterranean doors and windows from the Greek Islands to the Atlas mountains, and in Spain, from the Orange Blossom Coast of Valencia to the rias of Galicia. No artist captured the decorative capacity of the Spanish sky better than El Greco, who streaked his heavens with yellows and greens to create curtains of distant pigment.

The 'blue people' of Morocco, who with the Almoravids invaded the peninsula during the eleventh and twelfth centuries, considered blue the colour of the universe, the sacred colour of the firmament. In the sky of Spain they discovered a luminous spectrum, oscillating between the aquamarine glaze of Damascus glass and the depths of the blue-black Saharan night.

Green is the colour of fertility in Spain as elsewhere. But nowhere has it so many shades and transformations between valley and ocean. The natural viridian green of the Celtic north-west is the product of the soft Atlantic rain and the green of the land is at times so intense as to seem tropical. The apple green of the Basque country is different again, while in Andalucia the grey-green olive trees march in a dusty procession across the arid earth like files of soldiers. In Islam green is the sacred colour of the

Above The effects of light and shade have had a commanding influence upon many of Spain's greatest painters, in particular Velásquez, El Greco and Sorolla.

Left The colour purple was first extracted from murex snails by the Phoenicians off the Mediterranean coast. Vibrant oceanic colours have remained a vital force in coastal culture as can be seen in any Spanish fishing village.

Right Simple popular architecture and interiors are brought to life with traditional ceramics and glass, their bright colours accentuated by white-washed walls.

42

oasis and symbolizes community. Perhaps the preference for green paintwork against the white-washed houses of Extremadura derives from this.

In the end, however, the colours taken directly from nature are the most characteristic of Spain. The yellows, golds and saffrons hanging over the sierras at sunset; the delicate, tawny shades of *xerez* (sherry); the terracotta of the sandy earth of the Meseta, these are the shades that have become the adopted colours of the people. They are to be seen in the heraldic stone façades of Salamanca, in the great frescoes of El Escorial and in the Spanish flag.

During the 'Siglo de Oro', the golden age of sixteenth-century Spain, the gold and silver plundered from South America was melted down and hammered out to fill churches and palaces with the 'divine' sheen. Wood and metal were stamped with layers of gilt leaf; robes and tapestries sewn with precious thread. For a brief moment, these colours expressed both the temporal dominion and the

Tones of terracotta are the most constant colours seen in the interior regions of Aragón, Castile and Extremadura. From the soft copper hues of wicker drying in a barn near Cuenca to the burnt umber, rust red and bronze tones of leather, metal, stone, paint and pottery, these are the colours that best express the arid earth and fiery sun.

intense Catholicism of the Hispanic empire.

Saffron is the floral equivalent to gold. Each year for two short weeks the saffron harvest of Spain produces over half of the world's total crop. The mauve, bloodshot saffron crocus has long been associated with light and happiness. It is liberally used as a colouring agent in cooking, especially in *paella* and the other rice-based dishes of Spanish cuisine.

Saffron shades into the ochre yellow of the Spanish autumn. This is the season when the country is bathed in a soft, western light and the trees, vines and mountain sides of herbs and bracken turn through a blaze of rusting yellows and bronzing greens to become the black silhouettes of winter. It is the time when the wheat stubble is set alight and the earth burns in a mass of shimmering miniature sunsets.

Colour blows through every vent of Spanish life. It expresses celebration, mourning, joy, deprivation, anguish, love and death. It is an element embedded in the land, the architecture and the art.

Architecture

The spirit of Spanish architecture was formed during the centuries of reconquest. Romanesque, Gothic and Renaissance influences filtered in from France and Italy and were interpreted by the architects of Spain to fit the practical needs of the age. What defines this Christian architecture is a sense of permanence conveyed by sheer mass. Arab civilization, on the other hand, was a culture of recreation and reflection induced by the idyllic climate of Andalucia. African, Asiatic and oriental influences were all adopted by succeeding tribes of Moslem invaders and in the Mezquita, or great mosque, at Córdoba can be seen the origins of the Spanish love for decorative profusion. In the contrast between austerity and exuberant embellishment lies the commanding characteristic of Spain's architecture.

No one who journeys into the interior of the country can help but notice the sheer number and variety of distinctive buildings. Literally thousands of *castillos* litter the promontories of the Meseta; almost every hamlet in the Pyrenees possesses some exquisite example of Romanesque creativity; and streets of Renaissance palaces lie in dozens of old provincial towns. The dense, fragmented nature of Spanish architecture would take one person more than a lifetime to unravel.

Not only did the concurrent influences of Moorish and Christian culture produce such hybrid styles of architecture as Mozarabic and Mudéjar, but a complex web of influences caused the Gothic style, for instance, to develop in Catalonia in a different way from the same style in Castile. The history of Spanish architecture is an intricate subject dependent upon innumerable cultural forces, which does not form a simple coherent pattern of evolution.

It is much easier to comprehend the buildings by looking at how architectural form has been adapted by the various cultures of Spain to suit their needs and temperament. In so doing it becomes clear how deeply architecture mirrors not simply the attitudes of a particular age, but the enduring characteristics of the people and the land.

Take the Alhambra, the celebrated palace and fortress of the Moorish monarchs in Granada, built during the twilight of Arabian rule in the peninsula. To the millions of visitors who pass through its gates each year, the succession of courtyards and gardens somehow have an unreal cinematic quality which could easily be attributed to its restoration in the 1920s. But this, it is clear, was the original inten-

Left The earlier Roman ruins, with their many types and styles of column, provided the visual reference for the curious mixture of arches in the Mezquita, or mosque, at Córdoba.

Right and below The Moslem presence in Spain, which lasted for over seven centuries, exerted a powerful influence on Spanish architecture. The forest of arches in the mosque, the vivid patterns and ornamentation, remain a testament to the brilliance of Arab architects and their civilization.

Above Verses from the Qur'an, in stylized cufic writing, were damascened in precious metals around the mihrab, or prayer niche, of the mosque.

46

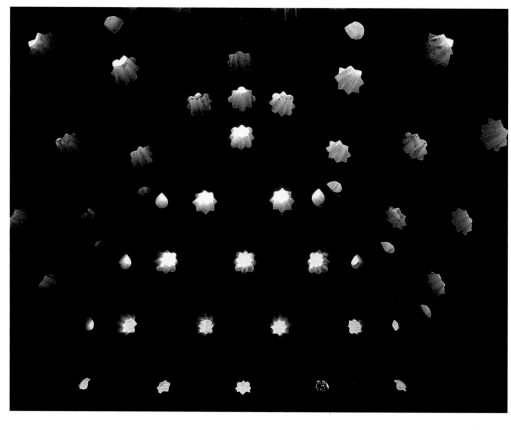

Above Delicately carved capitals and stucco work are a feature of the Alhambra. Soft bands of colour were sometimes applied to the stucco to enhance the stylized cufic script.

Above Filigreed ceilings in the Alhambra create an effect of architectural weightlessness. Moorish architects were continuously inventing new methods of supporting the elaborately decorated ceilings and some of their ingenious solutions, such as ribbed vaulting, were subsequently adopted by Christian builders.

Right The Moors believed they had found paradise in Al-Andalus and their architecture came to reflect that belief. A ceiling in the subterranean baths of the Alhambra was punctured with Islamic stars to create the illusion of night during the day.

Right A forest of marble columns – 124 in all – support the stucco walls of the Patio of the Lions.

tion. The early architects of the Alhambra devised a weightless structure which dissolved abstractly, like a flame, into the surrounding mountains.

The thin walls of ochre-red adobe had no defensive purpose but served rather as backdrops upon which the mantle of Islamic ornamentation could be hung. The Arabs were originally a nomadic people; and fresh waves of desert invaders constantly regenerated the civilization of Al-Andalus until the thirteenth century. Their architecture was based upon the tent, and the Alhambra is little more than an extended city of tents that has survived in its present form only by chance. As Titus Burckhardt remarked in *Moorish Culture in Spain* (trans. Alisa Jaffa, London, 1972): 'To the Islamic-Arabic mentality, to their consciousness of the transitory nature of things, the residence of a ruler is a home built for a limited period.' The Alhambra, ephemeral as it was, became a retreat for the Kings of Granada where they could relax between bouts of internecine feuds.

In the first instance, Islamic architecture was functional. Façades were on the whole plain in line with the teachings of the Qur'an which forbade outward expressions of ostentation. But the full imagination of Arab architects was released upon the interiors of palaces and houses. Through intense ornamentation they kept space in constant movement and manipulated the eye, as rhyme affects the ear in poetry, until the senses were lulled through the endless repetitions of pattern into a state of calm hypnosis.

In the Alhambra there is no axis around which the buildings relate. The Court of Myrtles, the Court of the Lions, the Chamber of the Kings and the Chamber of the Mozarabs flow, connect and disperse between patios, gardens and passageways like the delta of the river Guadalquivir – an illusion propagated through a delicate, sensual understanding.

The bright, metallic glow of tiled wainscotting was one way in which this effect was achieved. Endless interwoven arabesques, interlacing patterns and *lacerías* reflected the sublime cycles of nature. The abstract designs were not intended to nudge the imagination, as Western figurative art attempts to do, but to intoxicate the senses with a feeling of peaceful illumination through a constantly repeated pattern of movement.

Above the wainscot the arabesques continue in stucco friezes bearing decorative inscriptions. The cursive writing on the wall encircling the chambers and halls of the Alhambra read like metaphysical poetry; and the crowning glory of the inner chambers are the honeycombed ceilings dissolving like

47

Left Romanesque and Gothic monastic cloisters were decorated with intricately carved capitals, which provide a powerful insight into the spiritual symbolism lurking in the imagination of the time.

Right The pilgrimage route from Europe to Santiago brought with it the Romanesque and Gothic styles of the Continent, which were then disseminated southwards as the Christian reconquest won territories from the Moorish kingdom of Al-Andalus. The greatest stone mason of the Romanesque age was Maestro Mateo, who was responsible for the exquisite carvings around the cathedral of Santiago de Compostela. Over the centuries pilgrims have been greeted by the seated figure of St James the Apostle (above), wearing his crystal-studded nimbus. To guarantee a place in heaven, pilgrims place their hands in the holes to either side of the bust of Maestro Mateo (below), and bow their foreheads to touch his.

R*ight* Romanesque style reached into the farthest recesses of the country and new churches were often built over the ruins of earlier Moslem mosques, as was the case with the church of Santa Maria la Mayor in Trujillo, with its characteristic square belfry.

A*bove* Exceptional examples of Romanesque architecture exist in almost every village in northern Spain, where the church served as a place of worship and refuge. This function gave rise to a robust, defensive style which has remained a strong force in Spanish architecture.

F*ar right* During the thirteenth and fourteenth centuries Barcelona was the main port supporting the Aragónese-Catalan seaborn empire. Its prosperity was expressed through some exceptional Gothic architecture, built about the narrow streets of the Barrio Gótico.

Right The cross-fertilization of Islamic and Christian architecture gave rise to the vernacular style known as Mudéjar, typified by red brick decorated with tiles.

Above Teruel possesses the best collection of Mudéjar towers in Spain. Four church belfries formed gateways into the city and four towers were raised at intervals along the wall to serve as strategic look-out points.

Above right Mudéjar architecture flourished in areas such as southern Aragón and Toledo, where a strong Moorish presence remained even after the territories had been won back by the Christians. This detail of a tower in Teruel shows a simple Romanesque arch supported by ceramic columns.

mist to complete the impression of weightlessness.

Ironically, next to the Alhambra, and joined to it by a staircase, is the royal palace of Charles V, built by Mohammedan workmen in return for the privilege of continuing to wear their turbans. A heavy, despotic structure, it is an eloquent and potent transplant of the Italian Renaissance. Its muscular façade and interior circular court of Doric and Ionic columns are the antithesis of Moorish architecture.

In the long term, the Spanish spirit of austerity became the most characteristic feature of buildings. Spanish Renaissance architecture underwent two further stages of evolution from the Italian formula. First came Plateresque, a classical ornamental style, often so delicate that it resembles the work of silversmiths, or *platerías*, rather than of masons. What gives this style distinction is the flamboyant yet exact sense of detail seen to perfection in Santiago de Compostela at the Hostal de los Reyes Católicos, the royal hospital built for the pilgrims by the Catholic monarchs, Ferdinand and Isabella. Secondly, and of deeper significance for Spanish architecture, is the Herreran style, named after Juan de Herrera, whose masterpiece is the royal monastery of El Escorial.

El Escorial looms ominously beneath the grey boulder-strewn Sierra de Guadarrama, a few miles north-west of Madrid. It was intended to be the mausoleum of the Spanish monarchy, located at the centre of Philip II's unwieldy empire. Its vast symmetrical dimensions express in the language of granite the audacity of Spain's single-minded conquest and conversion of the New World, undertaken simultaneously with the Catholic Reformation in Europe. As the Alhambra mirrored Moorish visions of an earthly paradise, so El Escorial resounds with the memory of Hispanic imperial might: a private fantasy succeeded by a public vision.

At different moments each has been considered the eighth wonder of the world, and indeed there exist striking similarities between the two palaces. Both are built high up overlooking their rulers' kingdoms with façades remarkable for the lack of external pretensions. Philip II's order to Herrera for the construction of the monastic palace was short and sharp: 'Above all, do not forget what I have told you – simplicity of form, severity in the whole, nobility without arrogance, majesty without ostentation.'

El Escorial fulfilled Philip II's wishes exactly. Even the granite from which it was constructed has resisted the ravages of erosion from the biting winds, which blow off the Guadarramas from late autumn to the spring. Its rigid form is as quintessen-

La Giralda (literally 'weather vane'), the minaret attached to the cathedral in Seville, was built by Moroccan architects towards the end of the twelfth century. The restraint and elegance of the construction and the use of brick in the design were to typify Mudéjar work in succeeding centuries.

Right A long tradition of elaborate architectural decoration exists in Spain, partly due to Moorish influence. The fantastic nature of much Iberian architecture of the late fifteenth century earned itself the name Plateresque because its rich ornament resembles the work of silversmiths, or *platerías*. The House of Shells in Salamanca is an example, faced with scallop shells in allusion to the Knights of the Order of Santiago.

Below As the Moorish hold on the peninsula gradually diminished, Gothic churches and cathedrals rose in the expanding towns of the central Meseta. Spanish churches, such as the Church of San Martín at Trujillo, showed a love of lofty arcades made possible by new vaulting techniques that were explored to their limits.

54

tial to Spain's architecture as the interior exuberance of the Alhambra and appropriately provides a final resting place for the Spanish kings.

Spanish architecture becomes distinctive with the unique group of Pre-Romanesque palace-churches, which were built in Asturias in the wake of the earliest Christian resistance to the Saracen invasion of 711. These buildings adopted several features from the architecture of the Romans and Visigoths, and from the neighbouring Mozarabs to the south and Franks to the north-east. But Romanesque architecture relies principally for its effect upon the purity and simplicity of its style and proportions, and the delicacy of its stone carving. Spanish Romanesque is unquestionably one of the greatest, but most forgotten achievements of European architecture. In the isolated valleys of Aragón and northern Castile almost every hamlet, whether still inhabited or not, has a Romanesque church, sometimes in ruins, sometimes the only surviving monument: the cathedral of Roda de Isabena contains a surface area greater than the surrounding village. The profusion of Romanesque is such that some sees do not even possess complete listings of their possessions.

Early Romanesque constructions had to fulfil two

essential functions. First and foremost, they were places of worship where the local inhabitants met to pray, but as important as the spiritual factor was the defensive role of the church in protecting the community. As a consequence, Spanish Romanesque has a look of robust impenetrability – walls are massive with windows built high and narrow, and a square Lombard belfry was often incorporated into Catalan churches to serve as a look-out tower, emphasizing the church's militant function.

Inside a Romanesque building, the impression is of massive strength, while in a Gothic structure architecture achieves a sense of weightlessness, of soaring space. The Benedictine monks, who initiated the first great era of Romanesque building, gave life to their architecture with luxuriant carvings in the capital heads and the rich masonry around the exterior doors. Masons employed symbolism from every quarter. Biblical themes were portrayed eloquently with mythical monsters, with prophets and apostles, angels and demons, zoomorphic patterns and figures from daily life. However, these decorative tendencies were swept away in the twelfth century after the arrival of the austere Cistercian monks from France. As their apostle St Bernard of Clairvaux asked: 'What is the use of these

Above The interior of Salamanca's new cathedral was carved with equal delicacy, the soft quality of the stone hardening and turning golden with age. This Castilian town became one of the most progressive intellectual cities of Renaissance Europe.

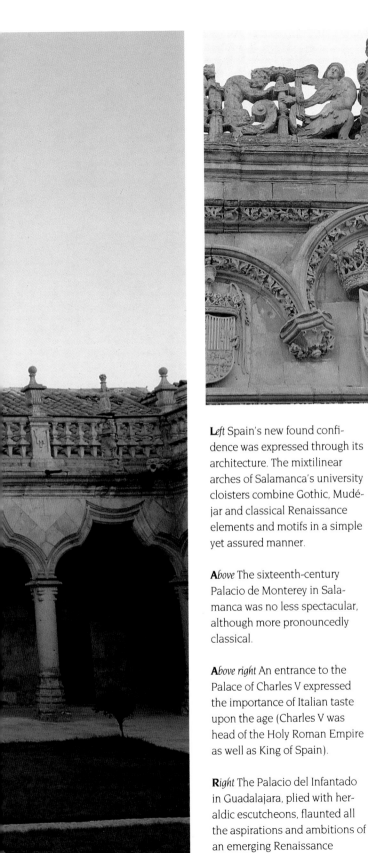

Left Spain's new found confidence was expressed through its architecture. The mixtilinear arches of Salamanca's university cloisters combine Gothic, Mudéjar and classical Renaissance elements and motifs in a simple yet assured manner.

Above The sixteenth-century Palacio de Monterey in Salamanca was no less spectacular, although more pronouncedly classical.

Above right An entrance to the Palace of Charles V expressed the importance of Italian taste upon the age (Charles V was head of the Holy Roman Empire as well as King of Spain).

Right The Palacio del Infantado in Guadalajara, plied with heraldic escutcheons, flaunted all the aspirations and ambitions of an emerging Renaissance family, the Mendozas.

ridiculous monsters, these ferocious lions, centaurs, tigers and soldiers in places where the people devote themselves to prayer and contemplation?' Consequently, Romanesque ornament took on a more sober, severe form which suited the Spanish ethos.

The sixty or so Cistercian abbeys in Spain, generally considered the most outstanding of their kind, became the vehicle for Gothic style, their interiors assuming lofty heights. The majority of Spain's seventy cathedrals are Gothic, with the few exceptions of Santiago de Compostela, the old cathedral of Salamanca, Zamora and Seo de Urgel which are Romanesque. The cathedral is the perfect medium of Gothic artistry, as Toledo, Burgos and the 'crystal house' of León exemplify.

The cavernous interiors of the great Gothic churches of Spain were built to make the altar accessible to the eyes of the great multitudes of worshippers. This was unquestionably the basic precept of the particular style of Gothic which developed step-by-step with the expanding Catalan-Aragónese empire during the thirteenth and fourteenth centuries. The quest for wide, uninterrupted space found its answer in the Catalan hall-church, where vaulting was taken to its logical limits to allow the priest and people to communicate without interference. The cathedrals of Barcelona, Palma de Mallorca and Gerona are all magnificent examples of this pure proportional technique.

But, without doubt, the most striking building of this era is the cathedral of Seville, the largest Gothic cathedral in the world. Its dimensions are so daunting that even the most resolutely non-believing twentieth-century tourist cannot but be moved. In 1401 the chapter of Seville agreed to raise 'a church so great that those who see it shall think we were insane'. Only St Peter's in Rome and St Paul's in London surpass it in size. The mosque which once stood on the site is gone, except for the Patio of the Orange Trees and the Giralda, the twelfth-century minaret now used as a belfry and weathervane.

Inside, the diffused Andalucian sunlight filters through the stained-glass windows and dances dimly among the superabundance of figurative sculptures, *retablos*, gilded *rejas* and rich religious paraphernalia. As your eyes adjust to the gloom, the clustered columns seem to rise like inner steeples into the empyrean. It is a true blend of Gothic ingenuity with Renaissance splendour, finished extravagantly with gold, the lavish gesture of Spain as a united Christian power at the head of a global empire.

Right A reaction to the fussiness of Spanish Baroque led to a revival in Neo-classic designs, as expressed by this spiral staircase in the monastery of Santo Domingo de Bonaval at Santiago.

Left and below The bullring at Ronda is the oldest in Spain and contains a magnificent twin-storey, arcaded gallery around the arena. This is where bullfighting on foot first developed. The simplicity of the design was clearly based on the Roman amphitheatre and influenced by the Neo-classic trends of the eighteenth century.

childrens
area.

60

But seven hundred years of Islamic influence had indelibly left its stamp on the Spanish psyche. The cross-fertilization of Mohammedan and Christian styles caused a vernacular form of architecture to evolve, popularly termed Mudéjar – a derivation of the Arabic world *mudijalat* meaning 'vassal'. Mudéjar developed in the hands of the large number of Moors who lived under Christian jurisdiction, but were allowed to continue their skills of carpentry, bricklaying and plasterwork. Examples exist throughout Castile and Aragón and are particularly concentrated in Toledo and Teruel. Mudéjar is distinctive for its use of brick and stucco and the synthesis of Arabic modes of decoration with Romanesque, Gothic and Renaissance principles of construction.

In the fourteenth century, Pedro the Cruel refurbished the Alcázar of Seville in imitation of the Alhambra. This started a vogue among the Spanish nobility for an exotic style of decoration within their palaces, which reflected an oriental sense of ease and comfort. Rooms were plastered with delicate stucco *lacerías*, enlivened with colourful glazed tiles and crowned with intricately inlaid *artesonado* ceilings. Mudéjar craftsmanship characterized Renaissance domestic architecture in Spain, and remained popular up until the end of the sixteenth century, especially in Seville where the Casa de Pilato is a perfect example of this utterly Spanish style.

But this fusion of Eastern and Western sensibilities was swamped at the beginning of the seventeenth century by the Baroque revolution imported from Rome. In Spain, the Baroque was soon transmuted into another phase of native decorative fantasy: seething façades of animated, ostentatious ornament faced light-and-shade filled buildings, like the palace of the Marqués de Dos Aguas in Valencia, with extravagant theatrical effects which continued to express Hispanic might.

The most exaggerated of these compositions were the work of the family of José de Churriguera and his disciples, described by Richard Ford, in his brilliant and vibrant writing, as follows:

> **T**he heresiarch of flagitious taste has bequeathed his name as a warning to mankind. El *Churrigueresco* designates all that is bad and vicious; those piles of gilded wood and fricassees of marbles, with which the old churches of Spain were unfortunately filled by a well-intentioned mistaken desire to beautify.
> (*Handbook to Spain*, London, 1845)

Far left Baroque architecture was a reaction against the formality of the Renaissance, and again indulged the Spanish love of decorative fantasy. The main disciples of the movement included José de Churriguera and Ignacio Vergara, the sculptor responsible for this highly fanciful entrance to the Palacio del Marqués de Dos Aguas in Valencia.

Left The portal of the palace, carved from translucent alabaster, is flanked by naked slaves who stand upon jars alluding to the two rivers – *dos aguas*. Above the door stands a Madonna and Child, surrounded by angels and streams of light.

62

This is unfair: the form known as Churrigueresque includes many memorable and beautifully executed buildings, including the Plaza Mayor in Salamanca.

Indeed, it is hard not to be intrigued by the utter excess of the form. The Transparente behind the high altar of Toledo cathedral, with its coils of chubby cherubs and ascending seraphs spiralling into the cupola, or the sacristy of La Cartuja in Granada, encrusted with ornamentation and borne aloft upon undulating Solomonic columns, are among the most intoxicating achievements of Spanish architecture.

In Spain, however, a severe reaction to Baroque began with the establishment of an academy of architecture in Madrid in 1744, whose French bias dictated an official style that was all too often sober, cold and ultimately expressionless. This bland Classical revival continued well into the twentieth century, challenged briefly by the exuberant originality of Modernism in Barcelona.

Spanish architecture is marked by phases of austere monumental building and outbursts of decorative fantasy, overlaid by a multitude of regional styles and local architectural ingenuity which illustrate the disposition of the people, their available materials and their way of life.

Far left Early twentieth-century exhibition architecture in the Plaza de España in Seville. Architectural features from almost every previous era have been adapted, and twin-columned arcading and decorated wooden ceilings mix effectively with Neo-classic windows and tiled balustrading.

Left The plaza was built specifically for the Ibero-American exhibition of 1929. Decorative paving, water and arched pedestrian bridges were all incorporated into the overall design.

Stone

Every Spanish city, every town, every village has a central plaza. It is the focus of activity, alive with the hum of civic commerce and presided over by the local patriarchs sitting around, watching the days rise and fall between shots of brandy and the odd hand of cards. Plaza life is the mirror of the community. No two are alike.

All the peculiarities of Spanish vernacular architecture radiate from the plaza; the thread-like white lanes of Andalucian villages, built tall and narrow to keep the houses shaded from the burning noon-day sun; the dim cobbled ghettoes where Jews and Arabs lived in cities which they had helped make great; streets of medieval and Renaissance palaces; the troglodyte gypsy quarters of Granada and Guadix.

Spain has been called 'a land of saints and boulders' and stone is the one common element in its vernacular architecture. Granite formed the villages strung out along the road to Santiago; the walls and battlements of the *castillos*, which christened the kingdom of Castile, were constructed of bricks and rubblestone; the golden sandstone cloisters of Salamanca were the rivals of Oxford quadrangles and the halls of the Sorbonne as centres of learning.

Deposits of rarer stone were used where possible in the adornment of palaces and churches, including the beautiful pink streaked marble of Alicante, onyx from Andalucia, alabaster from Aragón and serpentine from Almería, while granite has been carved in a thousand forms to create fountains, drinking troughs and benches. But it was the principles of Roman imperial engineering that implanted a lasting understanding of dimension, proportion and symmetry.

Roman architecture drafted from Italy and other parts of the Empire was inherently practical. The great aqueduct at Segovia, cutting across the city's skyline like a surreal stone horizon, marks the pinnacle of Hispano-Roman structural achievement. It was built without any binding agent, ashlar upon ashlar, and continues to this day to carry water into the heart of the city.

Travellers through Spain remark upon the 'cyclopean masonry' – the vast blocks of stone used so often in construction. The walls of Carmona, Tarragona and Lugo; the sixty arches of the bridge spanning the river Guadiana at Mérida; the ruined amphitheatre at Italica, were all structural ancestors of later medieval engineering which lent such a sense of strength to a people unable to find stability

The vast square towers of the *castillo* looming above Trujillo were built by the Moors. *Castillos* were normally erected not as single fortresses but as part of extensive defence lines.

Cyclopean granite blocks are
one of the great wonders of
Spanish architecture, especially
in Castile, León and Galicia. The
strong, indomitable nature of
this stone is peculiarly in keeping with the character of the
people.

Left Stone carving of the eighteenth century was inspired by the curvaceous nature of Baroque, but the intricacy of work was often dictated by the hardness of the stone rather than the skill of the carver.

Below Semi-circular stone steps are a common feature of both civil and ecclesiastical architecture of the Baroque age, especially in Galicia.

in their own political existence.

Towards the end of the Hispano-Roman era, Iberia had become a prosperous and vital limb of the empire. Many farms had been transformed into magnificent country estates producing wine, wheat and olive oil for exportation throughout the Mediterranean. Mosaics, frescoes and sculpture reached a level of colour and form equal to Italy itself and the peristyle, or colonnaded courtyard, which lay at the centre of most private mansions, was the inspiration behind the later Spanish patio. To succeeding invaders the Roman legacy was one which they adapted to their own needs, not least in the field of defensive engineering.

The *castillos* which grew up along the gradually shifting frontiers between the Moors and Christians had their antecedents in Roman city walls. The scale upon which they were built is magnificent. Jagged stretches of crenellated ramparts, parapets and towers continue to crowd the horizon, having survived relentless summers and winters of neglect. The tenth-century *castillo* of Gormaz, one of the oldest and most complete fortresses in the Western world, stretches for an unbroken third of a mile across a bleak bare hilltop overlooking the river Duero in the province of Soria.

It dates to the first age of *castillo* building undertaken by the Muhammedans, who fortified their cities with citadels (*alcazabas*) as at Malaga, Almería and Tarifa and whose Berber mercenaries constructed lines of defence to protect the northern territories of Al-Andalus. Many of these fortifications were variations on Byzantine architectural principles and would later influence many Christian military outposts.

By the twelfth century, Knights of the Orders of the Templars and Hospitallers began to erect magnificent church-castles, such as Loarre in the province of Huesca in Aragón. There exists no purer example of Romanesque military architecture. A curtain of walls and cylindrical towers surrounds the sides defended by an artificial, steep rock face. The *castillo* and church, hewn from a silver-yellow stone, are a symphony of turrets and towers punctuated by graceful *ajimez* or twin-light windows and embrasures which look south over the dry indented plain of the Ebro basin towards Saragossa. Loarre towers above the landscape like some imaginary refuge in an illuminated manuscript.

Equally majestic examples from Gothic and Renaissance times survive, but the most distinctive church-castles are those of Mudéjar descent such as the *castillo* at Coca, with its pink-brick turrets. Many of

68

L*eft* The narrow winding lanes of Albarracín to the east of Madrid exemplify a medieval village built within the confines of a large fortification. Its architectural character has hardly changed in the last 700 years; only the cobbled streets have grown smoother with age.

A*bove* Houses throughout the north were often built of roughly-hewn freestones and some walls date back to the eleventh and twelfth centuries and the great age of Romanesque expansion. In parts of Galicia and northern Castile, the art of freestone construction continues to this day.

L*eft* A similar medieval atmosphere permeates many villages of northern Spain, including Santillana del Mar, where the houses surrounding the central plaza are supported on large ashlar blocks and are faced with brick and timber.

Far left Complete villages were built of freestones in the northern sierras of Spain. Walls were generally thick to keep the heat in during the winter and out during the summer. Windows were often added at a later date.

Left Lichen breeds in profusion on granite ashlars in the fresh Atlantic air of the northern regions of Spain.

Below A niche, generally used for religious images, becomes the setting for a sculptural still-life when filled with the shards of broken terracotta water pots.

these Mudéjar fortifications were erected during the fifteenth century when the threat of the Moors had almost been extinguished; but the conflicts of the Spanish nobility had taken their place.

Almost two-and-a-half thousand medieval castles are scattered throughout Iberia and that figure is ten times greater when fortified works are taken into account, including those of the Roman and pre-Roman era. It seems strange, therefore, that the expression 'castles in Spain' should come to be an epithet for day-dreaming. Though undoubtedly many *castillos* had shortlived careers, their presence was hardly chimerical. They continue to dot the landscape, witnesses of a thousand years of forgotten conflicts.

A more continuous life animated the villages which spread beneath the castle walls throughout Andalucia, the sierras of the Meseta and the regions of the north. All were at some time frontier populations, scraping thin livelihoods from the land and

often granted special rights, or *fueros*, in return for the defence of a particular territory. The earliest houses were built defensively about the plaza. These communities were collectively known as *pueblos*. For centuries they were, and in many regions still are, the mainstay of the Spanish social system held together by the strong links of interrelated families. But the real strength of the *pueblo* was an ability to allow intense individualism to exist hand-in-hand with the co-operative spirit. At a later stage, as the *pueblo* expanded, the houses unfurled into a maze of lesser streets. Internally the houses follow a common arrangement. In the basement animals and mules were stabled with a few barrels of local wine left to ferment. The upper storeys were used for family living, while the attic served as a curing and salting room for hams and sausages.

Local materials naturally dominated the architectural character of the *pueblo*. Rough dressed granite, slate and ironstone were used in many of the oldest

villages, especially in the northern regions. In Cata-lonia easily-wrought freestones were preferred. Stunning examples of early Romanesque settle-ments are still preserved, the houses erected with the same sense of space to be found in the Catalan churches. In Aragón and Andalucia the inhabitants, following the persistent Moorish tradition, used brick, *pisé de terre* or a mix of brick and rubble stone, while in the south the walls were often limewashed to abate the heat and the flies.

A different and more civilized, but utterly Spanish, world existed in the rich Moorish cities of the south. Residential neighbourhoods grew up in many urban centres where powerful local families resided. This tradition was continued into the fifteenth and six-teenth centuries by the Spanish nobility in the mar-ket towns of Castile. Stone palaces and señorial mansions arose in hundreds of Spanish towns: the Infantado palace built for the Duque del Infantado, head of the Mendoza family, at Guadalajara; the palace of the dukes of Medinaceli at Cogolludo; and the Monterrey palace at Salamanca are three of the most spectacular examples. Other towns such as Riaza in Segovia and Sedano in Burgos have streets full of palaces, their granite façades weathered by the years, and only a stone escutcheon above the main entrance alluding to the original occupants.

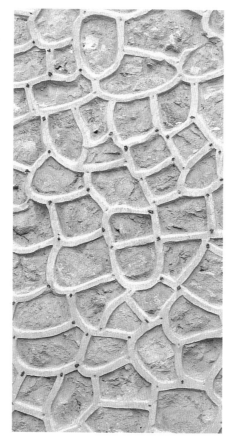

Esgrafiado decoration is exclu-sive to the city of Segovia, where this finish is often applied to exterior walls of houses in a var-iety of shapes and designs. This tradition most probably deve-loped from the custom of white-washing layers of mortar be-tween stones to form patterns.

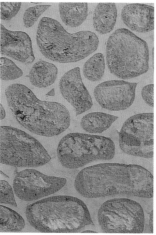

Right Cuenca is a vertical city with a variation in altitude of over 100 metres between upper and lower neighbourhoods. The Casas Colgadas, or 'hanging houses', positioned precariously above the gorge, date to the fourteenth century and appear to grow out of the rockface.

DETAILS

A manifold view

of the simplicity and flamboyance of

Spanish decorative arts. The vivid ingenuity of the potters,

smiths and carpenters is revealed through details –

from the brilliant, iridescent lustre

of Hispano-Moresque tiles to

the flowering of

Renaissance

ironwork.

Ceramics

Pottery has existed in various forms in Spain for the last four thousand years and unequivocably reflects the taste of every age. It is present in the primitive ornamentation of Neolithic earthenware; patios are adorned with the colourful patterns of Islamic geometric tiles or *azulejos*; palaces have rooms encased entirely in porcelain. Ceramics have remained a constant decorative element, ignoring social and religious barriers, and remain the nation's universal industrial art.

Tiles, whether glazed or unglazed, continue to be an important building material. In hot, insect-ridden climates their advantages are obvious. They are a cheap and cheerful substitute for marble, they appear cool to sight and touch even during the most sweltering heatwaves, and can be cleaned or replaced with little difficulty or expense. It is no wonder that their versatility bridges every corner of Spanish life. *Azulejos* are used profusely for the wainscotting of rooms and the tiling of complete walls, floors and staircases; on another level they are widely utilized as street signs, commemoration plaques or altar fronts.

Spain was a vital manufacturer of commercial pottery for the ancient world. Just outside Rome stands Monte Testaccio, a huge man-made mound piled high with the fragments of Spanish amphorae used in the transportation of vast quantities of oil and wine to the imperial capital. But it was the impact of the Arab invasion that was to change the course of western European ceramic art. Beneath the ruined Umayyad palace-city of Medina az-Zahra on the outskirts of Córdoba are the earliest excavated examples of European lustreware – shining metalliferous fragments, once part of complete vessels imported with rich silks and gold brocades from the cities at the eastern end of the Islamic empire, from Baghdad, Damascus, Constantinople and Alexandria. The bright and glossy iridescent finish has continued down to the present as the hallmark of Spanish ceramics.

Lustreware first developed along the banks of the rivers Euphrates and Tigris. Shiploads of tiles and jars were subsequently exported and traded for the minerals and foodstuffs of southern Spain. The bright metallic colours fulfilled a deep-rooted need in Islamic interior architecture, since the Qur'an outlawed the use of precious metals in decoration. The potter's art came as close as it could to the creation of a polished metallic finish. As Alice Frothingham, the authority on lustreware, remarks:

Shining metalliferous *azulejos* have remained a popular form of decoration since the Moors first introduced glazed tiles to Iberia over a thousand years ago. Many of the earliest arabesque patterns were later combined with Christian coats-of-arms as part of the design.

76

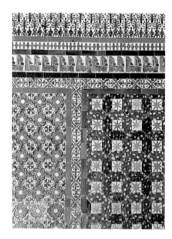

In Andalucia entire palaces, such as the Casa de Pilato, have been wainscotted throughout with richly patterned tiles, which help to cool the sweltering summer temperatures while adding another decorative dimension with their intertwining symmetries.

77

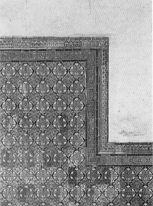

The Bisagra Gate, its pyramidal spires covered in green and white glazed tiles, forms an imposing entrance to the city of Toledo. Built for Charles V, it is one of the earliest examples of glazed roof tiling in Spain.

Since the sixteenth century Seville has maintained a strong tradition of tile-making, centred around the Triana quarter of the city. In the Plaza de España, glazing was effectively used to decorate architectural elements as well.

The most delightful feature possessed by the lustre glaze is the iridescent colouring that plays over it, flashing kaleidoscopically when the light or the angle of vision is changed, called *reflejos metálicos* by the Spaniards. Across the surface of darker lustres gleam rich blues, reds, purples and bronze while the paler metals reflect opaline green, lavender, blue, silver and gold.
(*Lustreware of Spain*, New York, 1951)

By the thirteenth century a thriving industry had developed in Malaga, initiated by migrant potters from Persia. Malagueña pottery became renowned throughout the Mediterranean and the wares were transported as far as England, Sicily and Egypt. The metallic recipes employed for glazing the earthenware remained a closely guarded secret from one generation to the next.

There were two main techniques. *Cuerda seca*, or dry cord pottery, employed blocks of bright manganese colour which were baked onto the biscuit and divided by black grease lines to prevent the colours from running together. This process was widely used in the early manufacture of tiles. The second technique, *loza dorada*, involved the use of a single colour, often with a gold background, over which designs were painted with quills or brushes. It was through the development of this technique that the Arabs created the exquisite wing-handled Alhambra vases, which once adorned the private garden patios of Granada.

For plates, goblets, vases, jugs and even tombstones, shapes were generally practical. But designs brought out the full creative imagination of the Arabs. Surfaces were festooned with intricate patterns, and principles of rhythmic repetition and perpetual symmetry guided the elaborate intertwining arabesques and interlaced ribbons. Cufic lettering and inscriptions, exaggerated, rounded, knotted and braided with soothing words such as 'absolution', 'eternity', 'happiness' and 'prosperity', were endlessly repeated around rims and edges; for the Moslems, like the Chinese, writing and lettering were invested with talismanic powers, similar to Taoist calligraphy. Words were used to communicate directly with God, to act as a constant reminder of the teachings of the Prophet. Certain words and phrases had a mantric quality and helped induce meditation and prayer. Hands were another symbol often painted onto objects: the outstretched hand, it was believed, could ward off evil spirits.

Ceramics seem to hold the essence of the Islamic

81

Left Narrow fillets of tile, or *verdu-guillos,* are often used as borders for shelving. This niche contains pieces of popular hand-painted ceramics, their simple designs accentuated by the bright patterns of the surround.

Below A collection of antique ceramic Spanish pots, jars and jugs decorates what was originally the kitchen in this Toledan *cigarral.* It has since been converted into a comfortable sitting-room where the family can gather around the large open fireplace in winter.

82

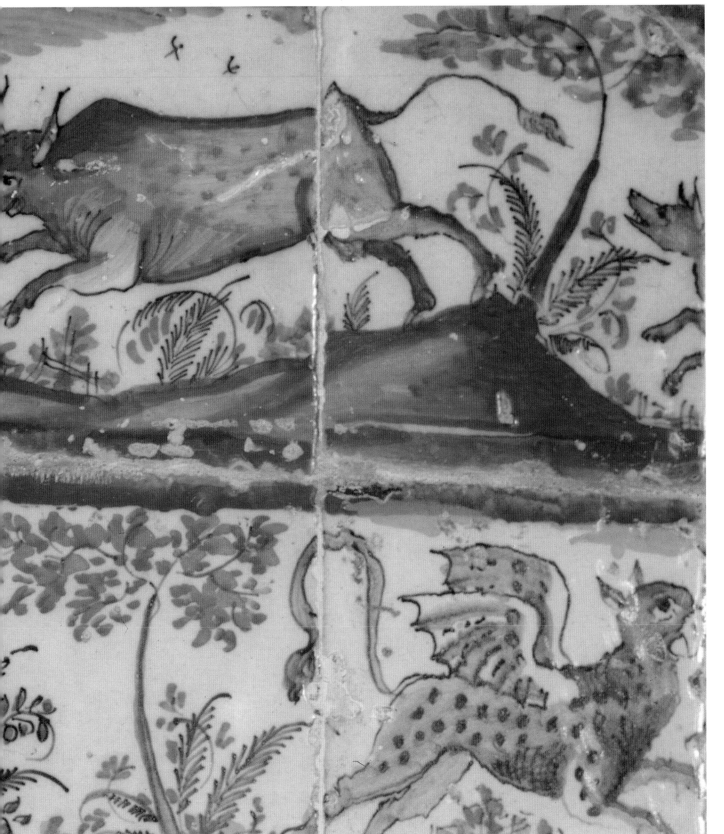

Left From the introduction of majolica tiling to Spain at the beginning of the sixteenth century, pictorial designs have immortalized many sides of Spanish life. A detail from a Talavera panel in the dining-room of an Andalucian palace depicts a bullfight and a mythical flight into hell.

83

Above Botes de farmacia, often painted with the coats-of-arms of the order to whom they originally belonged, were used for storing medicines in old pharmacy shops and are now prized objets d'art.

84

L_eft_ The framed seventeenth-century tiles on the wall of this Mallorcan farmhouse depict scenes and figures from Mallorcan life such as fishermen, washerwomen and labourers.

R_ight_ Spanish ceramic plates painted with animals, birds, floral designs or simple arabesque patterns are frequently used as wall decoration. These examples were produced mainly in the pottery shops of Catalonia and Valencia in the eighteenth and nineteenth centuries.

view of the world. Tiles and stucco lettering, inscribed with quotations taken directly from the Qur'an, wainscotted the walls of every Moorish palace and *alcázar*. Intricate patterns were individually coloured, fired and then fitted together like pieces of a jigsaw. Eight-pointed stars, formed by the superimposition of two squares, and other entangled motifs, in bright translucent tones, mirrored the constancy of the cosmos and the omnipotence of Allah.

Gradually ceramic art spread from Malaga and established itself in pockets of Aragón, Valencia, Catalonia and the Balearic Islands. As Idrisi, the twelfth-century Arab geographer, remarked: 'Here the gold coloured pottery is manufactured and exported to all countries.'

However, the demise of Arab sea power and trade in the western Mediterranean during the thirteenth century saw a migration of the Malagueños potters to Valencia. Manises and Paterna, now run-down suburbs on the way to Valencia airport, became the new industrial capitals. Here, Arabic designs mingled with Romanesque and Gothic influences filtering through from northern Spain. Once again, this cross-fertilization inaugurated the development of Hispano-Moresque pottery and lustreware. Without this cultural interaction, the history of European ceramic techniques and methods would have developed in a very different manner.

Valencian pottery was soon being exported to patrons in every part of Europe. As the eighteenth-century monk, Eximeno, put it:

> **T**he beauty of the gold pottery so splendidly painted at Valencia enamours everyone so much that the pope, and the cardinals and the princes of the world obtain it by special favour and are astonished that such excellent and noble works can be made of earth. (From *The Industrial Arts in Spain*, J. F. Riaño, 1879)

Christian motifs of flowers, human figures, heraldic shields, herringbone stripes and chequered squares gradually began to replace the arabesques. Figurations of birds, dogs, pigs, trees of life mingled with Gothic lettering and golden tracery. For two centuries Manises stood at the centre of this pottery empire.

But habits change, and after 1500, with the riches of the Americas and the change of focus towards the Atlantic, the colours became outmoded and the taste of the Spanish increasingly extravagant. Luxuries poured in from abroad. Elegant Venetian glass,

86

Below Tiled altars can be found in private chapels, churches and monasteries from Castile to Latin America, a practice which began during the fourteenth century. In this chapel arabesque tiles give a Mudéjar feel.

Left and far left Large square terracotta tiles are the most widespread form of flooring in the coastal areas of Spain as they remain cool even when submitted to direct sunlight and are easy to clean. They are still made from a mixture of clay and crushed almond husks, which is left out in the sun to dry after firing. Highly original effects can be created when clay tiles are interspersed with glazed and patterned designs on floors and wainscots.

Tiles work equally effectively outside as an element of garden design. The frog fountain in the Maria Luisa Park in Seville, a bright bench in the garden of the Casa de Pilato in Córdoba and a patio wall, serving as a vibrant background for large potted plants, all demonstrate the versatility of ceramic decoration.

Chinese porcelain, and gold and silver plate drove Hispano-Moresque pottery from fashionable tables.

An Italian monk, Francisco Niculoso, introduced a new method of tiling to Seville just as the news of Columbus's discovery was changing the city from a dirty, labyrinthine river port into a vast bustling commercial centre with a trade monopoly with the New World. This was *majolica*, or freehand picture tile painting, and with it several new colours including Seville orange, lemon yellow, sepia, magenta and emerald green entered the palette of Spanish ceramics.

Tile painting spread through every institution of southern Spain. Mile upon mile of tiled wainscotting, shimmering with Renaissance motifs and designs, was ordered for government buildings, convents and monasteries. Altar embroideries, *retablos* and complete sides of churches were replaced by *azulejos* painted with religious compositions. Some of the most exceptional examples of Spanish majolica work are to be found in South America.

The *cuenca* method of tile manufacture now replaced *cuerda seca*. For this, the craftsmen used a wooden matrix to stamp coloured designs into the face of the wet tile. Ceramicists were elevated to the level of painters and as the art matured, designs of Flemish tapestries – widely admired in Spain – were transformed into vast canvas-like panels of *azulejos*. Biblical themes adorned tiles exported to the new colonial settlements. Trade thrived; many new churches, such as Puebla in Mexico, were covered, outside and in, with profuse and colourful decoration. As Bernard Bevan described it:

> The brightest colours imaginable were applied to façades and domes ... brilliant domes, red, blue, yellow or white, sometimes even striped in Chevron patterns, are the most striking feature of churches in this region. *Cholula* itself, with more than fifty churches for less than five thousand inhabitants, is a sight not easily forgotten. In villages which were unable to build so expensively, church façades were painted to resemble tiles.
>
> (*History of Spanish Architecture*, first published 1938)

Popular commercial demand was met by the factories which began to develop in the towns of western Castile, especially at Talavera de la Reina, the original catalyst of this new industry. Today, it is a dust-blown town on the main road between Madrid and Extremadura. But every other dilapidated shop

continues to sell the bright vivacious pottery. The name of Talavera is still a household word in every Spanish family.

Talavera pottery rose to fame rapidly at the beginning of the seventeenth century, when a silver shortage hit Spain. The brightly coloured, freehand ceramics soon became as acceptable at the table of a nobleman as in the humblest wayside inn. The aesthetic appeal of Talavera pottery lies in its simplicity. Writers and poets continually referred to it in their literature and verse, while the great still-life painters immortalized the designs on canvas. For example, in the paintings entitled *Piece of Salmon, a Lemon and Three Vessels* and *Pomegranates, Apples, Jars and a Box of Sweetmeats*, from a series by Luis Meléndez, the vessels were most likely from Talavera. (These works were commissioned for a room at the palace of Aranjuez to illustrate the variety of food produced in Spain.)

The innocent pastoral scenes and enlivened sketches of rabbits, hares, storks and other animals, mixed with simple Renaissance patterns, had a virtually universal appeal. The advantages of an almost mass-produced pottery were obvious. It cost next to nothing to produce and was easily replaceable. It has therefore remained in production ever since. Talavera's continued success has been due to an ability to adapt to the changing needs and tastes of

Left and right Early Talavera potters created picture tiles relating popular stories of the age. In the nineteenth century industrial tiling was used for more commercial purposes such as colourful advertising on shop fronts.

91

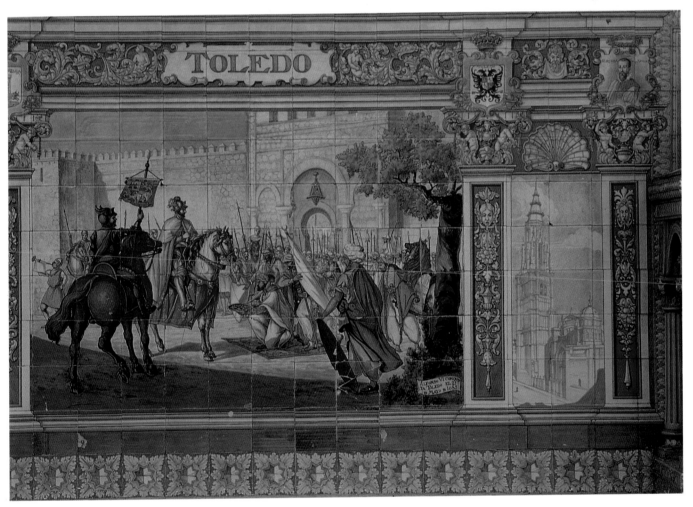

Right A detail of the Toledo picture tile in the Plaza de España in Seville depicts the surrender of the city to the Christians in 1085.

92

the time, and colours were constantly refined as ceramic methods were improved.

Shapes remained practical and covered the complete spectrum of domestic necessity – bottles, candlesticks, pharmacy jars, ink wells, sauce boats, plates, dishes, cups, bowls, fonts, wall basins, *aguamaniles*, and of course, *azulejos*. All were made to measure with coats-of-arms, quotations and lively drawings as required. The art spread into every area of commercial and private life; and would eventually be used as a medium for advertising.

By the late eighteenth century, French methods of *faïence* glaze inaugurated a new phase of *loza fina*, or fine quality, ceramics. The new age was initiated by the 9th Condé de Aranda, who had inherited a small pottery factory at Alcora in the mountains of Valencia. He sent artisans to Sèvres and Paris to learn the new art of porcelain manufacture, and within a few years a thriving industry had been established.

The popularity of Alcoran *loza fina* was immediate and widespread, and a graceful Spanish Rococo style developed. Charles III subsequently patronized a royal porcelain factory in the Buen Retiro Park in Madrid. The workmanship between the French and Spanish craftsmen of this period is often so similar as to make their work indistinguishable. But the War of Independence put an end to all that. Napoleon's troops occupied the factory in 1808 and a few years later, the British forces burnt it to the ground.

Of all Spain's industrial arts, pottery, ceramics and tile-making have remained the most deep-rooted. In every region without exception pottery plays some role whether practical, aesthetic or religious. Travelling through the country, it is impossible not to marvel at the enormous earthenware vats, or *tinajas*, standing like Ali Baba jars beside the road. Their use for the fermentation and storage of wine has, in many places, been superseded by modern methods of viniculture. Most have been put out to grass to serve as gargantuan flower pots, or even to convey directions to a nearby restaurant or hotel.

These extraordinary shapes and radiant lustres, which have developed from basic practical needs, express the Spanish celebration of movement and the flow of life. The Moorish arabesque and the free naturalistic line of the Talavera potter have been copied down to the present day. Innocently reflecting changing tastes through colour, line and form, the ceramic tile is a universal feature from the humble Andalucian homestead and the colonial monasteries of South America to the luxury modern villa.

The versatility of ceramic tiles as a decorative finish even extends to the staircase. Tiles serve utilitarian ends equally well as water carriers, basins or simple storage jars for medicines as at the pharmacy of the Hospital de Tavera.

Ironwork

From the earliest times, the rich deposits of metal beneath the Spanish earth have acted as a magnet to Mediterranean peoples. The material progress of Spanish civilization was inextricably linked to its wealth of gold, silver and iron reserves, which were also to influence the artistic and industrial development of the country.

It is said that trade with the peninsula was so profitable for the Phoenicians that they could afford to forge their anchors from gold and silver, exchanging them for eastern luxuries like ivory and alabaster. Certainly the Iberian kingdom of Tartessus grew opulent from extracting the precious ores from the hills surrounding the river Tinto in western Andalucia. These deposits remain productive to this day, making them the oldest operative mines in the world.

So developed were the methods of the Celtic ironsmiths by the second century BC that the Roman legions adopted the short bladed Celtiberian sword as their standard weapon of combat after the defeat of the Carthaginians in the second Punic war. The armoury business introduced by the Visigoths into their capital at Toledo has continued through to the present, albeit transmuted to a domesticated form. The silver road, or *via de la plata*, of the Romans was the route along which these metals were transported to the Atlantic seaboard and from there by boat to other parts of the empire.

Spain's metallurgical history has affected every age and every part of the country, but it is iron which is somehow most in character with the people and has remained the most distinctive of their metals. Spanish ironwork, in terms of both quantity and quality, is unsurpassable, and much can still be admired in its original position.

Iron symbolized the virility of the Christian crusade and became, in a sense, the adopted metal of the reconquest. The Moors preferred the nobler metals working gold, silver and especially bronze with files, saws, drills and vices. They were skilled in the art of damascening, but had little use for the smith. For the Christians, however, iron had an invincible, unpretentious practicality essential to their needs. An easily mined supply could be had in the northern sierras.

The earliest forges developed along the basin of the river Ebro, in the verdant recesses of the Cantabrian mountains and secluded valleys of the Basque lands. Spanish iron varies greatly according to geography. The black hue of the iron mined in the

94

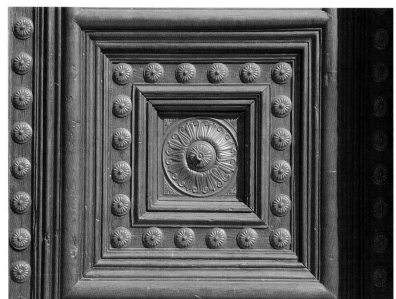

The ingenuity of the Spanish ironsmith found fullest expression in the decoration of doors and the construction of church *rejas*. The iron *verja* surrounding the tomb of Bishop Diego de Anaya, in the old cathedral of Salamanca, exemplifies the great skill of these early smiths, who from formless mass hammered out exquisitely delicate shapes.

The filigree designs of iron gates, such as these in Salamanca, developed from the long tradition of *reja* makers, whose work achieved greatest distinction in Spain's great Gothic cathedrals and churches. Elaborate screens were fashioned to protect the side altars and chapels whilst allowing the congregation to see through the bars into the interior.

Decorated nail heads and intricately worked *aldabas* (simple rings with highly decorative backplates) form a distinctive embellishment on doors.

R*ight* The Puerta del Perdón or Door of Pardon leading into the mosque at Córdoba is one of the most magnificent examples of door art in Spain. Hammered out from sheets of bronze and copper imprinted with Gothic inscriptions, the design follows a typically Moorish pattern and was probably the creation of Mudéjar craftsmen.

96

Atlantic regions turns purplish in the Basque provinces and a dark brown when refined from the ore extracted from the Catalan Pyrenees.

It was in Catalonia that the first forges in Europe evolved, with a capability of smelting quantities of pure iron. The adaptation of the hydraulic forces of the mill wheel created the constant current of air needed to heat the metal to the required levels of plasticity, so that form and shape could be hammered out of the solid. Rust was inhibited by dipping the red incandescent iron into oil, thus coating the metal with a water resistant layer.

The Spanish ironsmiths became veritable alchemists, turning the densest, most intractable of metals into weightless designs of gracious extravagant beauty; forging works of art from formless mass; and mastering the most unyielding type of matter in a way unequalled anywhere else. Iron became a medium in which the victory over Islam and the conquest of the New World were monumentally realized. For the indomitable character of the material seemed to reflect something of the spirit of those who colonized with cross and sword.

The ingenuity of the ironsmith excelled in the construction of the *reja* – the chancel screens which separated side chapels from the main body of a cathedral or church. Their purpose was to protect altar treasures while allowing as much vision as possible to those on the outside. The beauty of their form and the almost inexhaustible variety of their shape make them one of the glories of Spanish art. They were to affect every aspect of ironwork as it evolved into secular designs such as balconies, gates, lanterns and window grilles.

The earliest examples of *reja*-making can be traced back to the scroll patterns entwined into the general arabesques of Romanesque grilles. But the art was refined during the era of Catalan Gothic splendour. In the dim light of Barcelona cathedral, in the numerous side chapels surrounding the nave and cloistered garden, it is possible to discern the earliest naive manifestations of *rejeria* castings. Gothic traceries and architectonic bars crowned by gnarled spikes speak of the shrewd practicality that epitomized the Aragónese-Catalan empire.

By the fifteenth century the Spanish smith had developed his skills to extraordinary levels of architectural finesse. Cathedrals often held contests, similar to architectural competitions of today, to elect the most suitable *rejero* for a given side chapel, and wooden replicas were dummied up so that a winner could be commissioned. J. Starkie Gardner wrote of the *reja*:

L*eft* Doors were often plated with thin layers of copper fixed with iron nails, which have graciously oxidized over the centuries.

R*ight* Looking through from one courtyard to another in the Casa de Pilato, the delicate wrought-iron gateway acts as a veil, disguising the view to come. A typical Andalucian lantern hangs overhead.

Iron was widely adapted as an architectural fixture serving both practical and ornamental purposes, as manifested by these twisted chimneys in Cuenca; the *reja* gate surrounding the Puerta de la Gloria at the cathedral of Santiago de Compostela; and a circular balcony running around the corner window of a palace in Trujillo.

[It has] so grand and impressive a character as to confound all our previous conceptions of the material. The limits that its stubborn nature and the technical difficulties of the craft seem to impose are disregarded, and, in contemplation of the colossal rejas in the great Spanish cathedrals, it is hard to realise that effects in iron must be got swiftly by the hammer and punch while the iron is hot, or tediously by the file and chisel and drill while it is cold.
(From *Ironwork*, 3 vols., London, 1930)

What made ironwork the most Spanish of industrial arts was the fact that there was no parallel elsewhere in Europe. With no Italian prototype to follow, decoration had no standard and an utterly Spanish style developed. At a later stage Renaissance motifs, such as medallions, *amorini*, cresting and tracery, were adopted, but only as details within a thoroughly Spanish design. Later still, foreign artists adopted these same skills and methods.

Above all, the embellishment is distinctively Spanish. The delicate uniform working of the colonnettes, bars and columns; the gilded damascene

work so notable in the cathedral of Seville; the refined foliation and exquisite cresting which reached a zenith before the altar in the cathedral of Granada. There, the broad ornamental frieze which runs across the top of the *reja*, towering above the inanimate marble tombs of the Catholic monarchs, the *Reyes Católicos*, is composed of half-life-size figures dancing in a fleeting silhouette of grace and mystery. For a moment, the iron seems as ephemeral as a long Castilian shadow.

The art of the *rejero* passed down into industrial and practical smithery in numerous ways. The ornate standing candelabra and chain-suspended oil lamps; hearth accessories and firedogs, called *morillos* or 'little Moors' in Castilian; brasiers, that unique Spanish method of combatting the cold by filling a bowl with smouldering olive stones and placing it beneath a table skirted to the ground.

At some point in its evolution, iron touched every corner of the decorative arts in the adornment of doors, windows and furniture and in the construction of tables and chairs. Engraved appliqués were used to embellish the surfaces of chests and *bargueños*, and intricate experimentation by locksmiths opened up new fields in forged iron mechanisms.

By the end of the seventeenth century, there was a lull in the use of iron and with the invention of coke by Abraham Darby and the development of mass production, smithery turned from a craft into an industry. But the Spaniards never ceased to use it for the decorative purposes perfected during the Renaissance, and in Catalonia there was a brilliant revival of this art form during the years of Modernism.

The respect of the Spanish people for ironwork was graphically expressed in 1808, as the French forces marched south from Madrid to capture Toledo. The citizens felt such concern for the great gold-plated *reja* surrounding the high altar that they painted it black – and black it remains to this day.

Over the years Spain has been robbed of much of its heritage – by the French, and in this century by unscrupulous dealers. But the heritage of Spanish ironwork has remained, especially that of the *rejas*, their sheer weight preventing easy transportation.

Renaissance ironwork reflects like nothing else the superhuman endeavour of the Spanish during the years of colonial expansion – a mastery of form, dimension and artistry which no age has subsequently been able to emulate. Even today, in some of the more isolated communities of Castile there exists both a blacksmith and an ironsmith in villages with less than two hundred inhabitants.

102

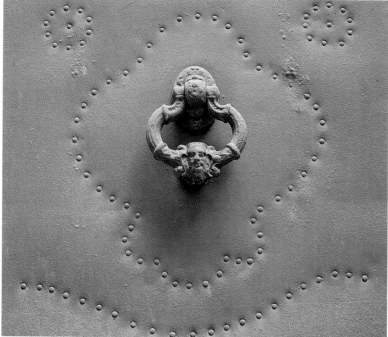

Left A simple scroll *reja* has been elegantly worked into an impenetrable window grille. *Rejas* are a common fixture on exterior windows throughout the country – a tradition first introduced by the Arabs who closely guarded the interior privacy of their houses.

Above and left Nineteenth-century door knockers were often forged from industrial iron. Sometimes the original door pattern designs were recreated with small tacks which traced the path of the former nailheads.

Left The boldly decorated entrance doors to a palace combine strong bands of decorated nailheads with elegant *fleur-de-lys* hinges. Door art is often indicative of the interior beyond.

Wood

Driving through Castile today it is hard to envisage the primaeval woodland which once covered the whole of Spain's central Meseta. An immense forest was slowly thinned and felled from the fifteenth century onwards, to clear a wider grazing route for the transhumant sheep on their seasonal migrations from one end of the tableland to the other. Timber was also widely employed in the construction of cities, for the ships of Spain's immense navies and as fuel to feed the hearth of every home through the winter.

Spain was once rich in a variety of indigenous trees such as walnut, oak, chestnut, Spanish cedar, red Mallorcan pine, olive and fruitwoods. From a very early date these competed with exotic species from Asia, Africa and the Americas: acana, terebinth, boxwood, ebony, rosewood, sandalwood and, of course, mahogany, the most widely used of them all.

But it is the delicate inlay and marquetry (*taracea*) introduced by Arab craftsmen, from which the arts of carving and polychrome developed, which distinguishes Spanish woodwork as a decorative medium. This strong tradition can be first discovered in the great Mudéjar *artesonado* ceilings of cities like Seville, Granada and Toledo. Polychrome carvings exist in various states of deterioration throughout the country, from the smallest half-ruined village church with an altarpiece riddled with woodworm, to the Museum of Catalan Art in Barcelona, where the most exceptional examples of Romanesque and Gothic sculpture are preserved.

Philosophy, not figurative symbolism, lay at the root of all Islamic art forms and it was geometry and intricate patterning that typified the work of the Moorish carpenters. Ibn Al-Makarri, the chronicler of the *History of the Mohammedan Dynasties in Spain*, wrote a rich description of the ninth-century *mihrab* (the prayer niche that shows the direction of Mecca) in the mosque at Córdoba:

> It was made of ivory and exquisite woods such as ebony, sandal, Indian platan, citrus and aloë. Formed of thirty-six thousand pieces fastened together by gold and silver nails, encrusted with precious stones. Its construction took a team of carpenters seven years to complete.

The numerical precision in this account is characteristic of all Moorish marquetry, and carpenters of Morocco still produce 'Granada Work' of star-patterning inlaid with mother-of-pearl, bone and

Artesonado ceilings are the crowning glory of many palaces built between the fifteenth and seventeenth centuries. The intricate geometric patterns were the work of Mudéjar carpenters who inlaid their star patterns with fillets of rare wood. The *artesonado* varied in shape from inclined octagons to semicircular cupolas known as *media naranjas* (half oranges) or delicately carved, flat-beamed structures.

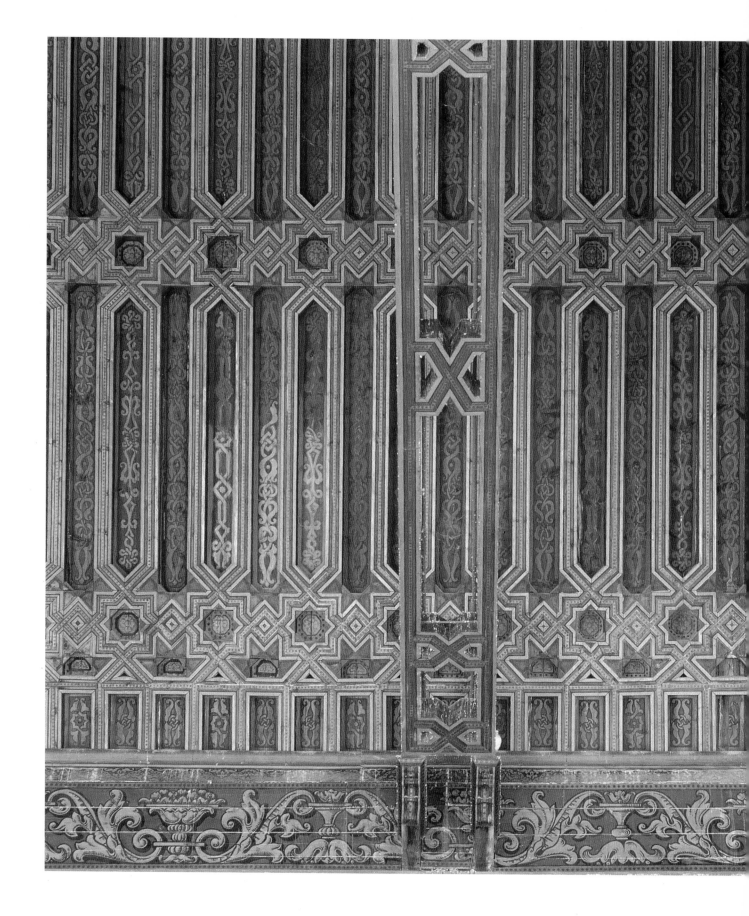

The *artesonado* became a digni-
fied expression of Renaissance
nobility and enhanced a feeling
of status and stateliness. After
the expulsion of the Moors from
Spain in 1610, coffered ceilings
were often polychromed, creating the effect of a sumptuous
jewelled casket.

boxwood, a form used extensively by the Saracen craftsmen of Al-Andalus to decorate boxes, chests and furniture. This preference for small pieces of wood no doubt arose from the scarcity of trees in Arabia. The inlay is intense like the light emitted by the galaxies on a clear Andalucian night.

The profoundest expression of this art is defined by the *artesonado* ceilings which can be discovered in churches and palaces throughout Spain; where the full mathematical ingenuity of the Mudéjar craftsmen can be appreciated. The ceiling represented one more area where the vision of paradise on earth could be created. There is a story of a Yemeni ruler, who built himself a vast palace in an oasis, with a roof modelled in opaque alabaster through which he could watch the clouds and birds passing overhead. The square of sky above an inner patio represented a private piece of heaven to the owner. Likewise, the decorated wooden ceiling was a worldly manifestation of the eternity of the cosmos. When Islamic philosophy and mysticism were replaced by the humanist values of the Renaissance,

The earliest surviving examples of Spanish furniture were commissioned by the church and consist mainly of chests and benches, carved with simple patterns or Gothic lettering. Wood was frequently covered with red velvet or leather fixed with brass nails, or otherwise painted.

the dark stained ceiling hanging above the bright white walls of the Spanish interior produced a stately, solid impression perfectly reflecting the dignity required by status. Thus, the *artesonado* became an essential decorative accompaniment of nobility.

Throughout the fifteenth and sixteenth centuries the art of the *artesonado* and coffered ceiling excelled. There is no doubt that many of them were made by Mudéjar carpenters, although some of the bright and more figurative polychrome finishes were probably executed by the local Pintor de Imaginería. Arthur Byne and Mildred Stapley, who photographed and wrote the classic account of *artesonados* at the beginning of this century, divided coffered ceilings into four categories as follows:

> It was either flat, simply beamed or coffered; or it was an open timber framing with elaborate tie-beams and double hip-rafters; or it was of three equal planes; or lastly, very polygonal in section, producing the effect of a barrel vault or dome. This last form, called a media naranja (half orange), was used over stair-wells and square rooms.
>
> (From *Decorated Wooden Ceilings in Spain*, 1920)

Dazzling examples of all these types exist in the great Mudéjar strongholds of Spain, Seville, Toledo and Granada, but some of the finest representations are to be found in more obscure locations like the Monasterio de Santo Domingo de Silos in Burgos, the Palacio del Infantado in Guadalajara or the university of Salamanca.

The complex arithmetic patterning was set forth in the *Book of the Carpenter* written in 1633 by a Sevillian nobleman, Diego López de Arenas. He described the intricate jigsaw-like laws of interlacery which emanated from the eight-, ten- and twelve-pointed stars governing the central structures. The work was regularly reprinted until the nineteenth century, which considering its technical nature, proves the enduring attraction of the *artesonado*.

Mudéjar carpentry lay behind Spain's first original period of domestic furniture design. Marquetry was lavishly employed to embellish 'hip' chairs and *bargueños* from the fifteenth century onwards. Before that time the itinerant life of the Spanish court demanded tables and chairs of a makeshift and easily dismantled nature. What has survived was originally commissioned by churches and ecclesiastical foundations and was built to a rather common formula. Tables were on the whole plain and heavy with splayed legs supported by wrought iron bars. Chairs were rectangular, of the *frailero* or 'mission' type,

110

Spanish furniture does not possess the same strong identity as that of England or France, and generally it is a sense of robust simplicity that characterizes much craftsmanship. Yet the influence of European fashions on Spanish cabinet-makers' designs can be felt through every age.

covered in velvet and secured by brass nails. The bench and stool were the only household items of any importance, their form generally simple and severe.

The chest, in its varying states of sophistication, remained up until the eighteenth century the one indispensable domestic chattel. Early flat-top examples were used as benches and the wood normally carved, painted or covered with cloth or leather secured by iron appliqués. The most famous example now resides in the cathedral museum of Burgos. This was the chest which El Cid filled with sand to deceive the Jewish money-lenders.

Again on a domestic level, a small wooden casket, or *cofrecito*, was frequently placed on tables as a practical ornament. As life in Spain became more settled the chest developed into the *bargueño* – the most quintessential piece of Spanish furniture and the single true invention of the Renaissance carpenters. The *bargueño* is a chest supported on a trestle table or solid cupboard, with two horizontal arms which pull out to support the front of the upper part, and can be used as a desk or cabinet for documents. When the front flap and doors are opened the inside reveals a hive of drawers and compartments for storing letters and small personal belongings. In decorative terms it ranged from simple lineal carving to rich, inlaid extravagance employing columns and colonnettes, repoussé ironwork, stitched velvet, even small dramatic scenes.

Walnut remained the most widely used wood until the eighteenth century, when mahogany was imported in bulk from the Colonies. Once again, iron was frequently applied for both structural and decorative purposes.

The tradition of carving, established by the Gothic choir-stall carpenters, has remained the conclusive Spanish signature for all finer pieces of furniture, from the robust decoration of a massive armoire to the lighter arabesques of a Rococo console table or the geometric detail of a fireplace, attributed to Gaudí.

Otherwise, furniture inevitably moved in step with the architectural style of the times. In the eighteenth century the Baroque style stressed a sense of theatricality, epitomized by the Salamantine architect and cabinetmaker José de Churriguera. In furniture, line was thrown to the wind and the underlying Spanish rigidity was turned into fantasy with twisted and erratic forms.

A sense of classicism was restored during the reign of Charles III whose Neapolitan education together with the recent discoveries at Pompeii heralded Italian fashions. The Bourbon Rooms in the royal palace of El Escorial display rich Flemish and Spanish tapestries on every available inch of wall, and there is a lighter atmosphere as elegance became the order of the day.

Of this period the most important figure was undoubtedly Ventura Rodríguez. His architecture and furniture designs were to affect every aspect of taste. Carpenters began to turn out commodes, cupboards, brightly coloured wooden chandeliers, dressing tables, bureaux and cornucopia mirrors for the provincial nobility. Comfort was sought after, and covered sofas were copied to designs being produced by the English in the Balearic Islands.

But this style changed almost overnight as Napoleon's armies marched in across the Pyrenees. French Empire mahogany furniture, stamped with gilded bronze decoration, was produced on a huge scale in the workshops of Madrid, Catalonia, Valencia and Andalucia.

With the popular decline of the style in the second quarter of the nineteenth century no ordered development of Spanish furniture followed. Workshops adopted a pastiche of styles: Empire, Isabelline or Victorian and Romantic. Ostentatious imitations with limited originality were churned out to meet the demands of a society in the process of gradual degeneration. Only in Catalonia, through the Modernismo movement, did design once again flourish in an original way.

The inconstancy created by regionalism undoubtedly had an effect on any uniform maturing of Spanish furniture design. And craftsmen were often employed on the construction of altarpieces to the exclusion of all other work. There are of course exceptions: the marquetry work of the Mudéjar carpenters and the exceptional Gothic carving of cathedral choir stalls are traditions of excellence in their own right. But what has always typified Spanish furniture design, on a popular level, is its solidity of structure and crude craftsmanship. In that form it possesses an unmistakable personality of its own.

115

Windows

Something of the character of every building in Spain, whether a farmhouse, a *castillo* or a cottage, can be gleaned by scrutinizing the exterior embellishment of the windows and doors which bear witness to the creative and imaginative powers of local craftsmen, the heirs of deep-rooted regional traditions.

A walk through an isolated *pueblo* or the old neighbourhood of any town or city, such as the Barrio Santa Cruz in Seville, will demonstrate the significance of the window as an exterior reflection of the household. Every year, competitions are held at hundreds of local village fiestas to judge the most colourful, well-arranged and sumptuously pot-planted balcony. To amble along the narrow lanes of a *pueblo* at fiesta time with every wrought iron or wooden balcony lovingly bedecked in cascades of geraniums, daisies, roses and lilies is an unforgettable sight. The slatted blinds and shutters glisten with a new coat of paint, the richly contrasting colours offset against the chalk white walls.

At other times of year, the balcony is used as a place to hang the washing, to put out the peppers and the corn to dry, or as a simple shaded terrace on which to watch the sun go down in the cool of the

Variations in the style and size of window designs have developed as a response to the strong sun of Spain. Any excess light is dispersed and filtered in a multitude of different ways – through alabaster tracery, iron bars and between slender colonettes of delicate *ajimez* windows.

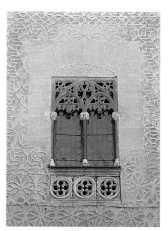

Flowers and cacti are characteristic of many outside balconies,
which cascade with colour at
fiesta time when competitions
are held in the villages to select
the most lovingly tended window display.

119

evening breeze; it is an extension of every garden and a living celebration of the window.

Spanish windows are different in that they almost inevitably open onto the inside of a room. Those exposed to the street are generally smaller than windows opening into interior patios and more often than not are protected by window *rejas*.

The window *reja* serves first and foremost to safeguard the security of a house, a tradition originally introduced by the Moors, whose houses invariably looked inwards to domestic privacy, but continued by their successors and a habit which has remained strong to this day.

By the fifteenth century, the art of the *reja*-makers had been so refined that windows on any level were often protected by their exquisite workings in iron. Apart from reasons of decorative symmetry, it is not easy to work out why there was any need to bar upper storey windows. One long held and slightly preposterous belief claimed that iron bars absorbed heat and kept rooms cool!

Another, more likely theory was put forward by Julian Pitt-Rivers in *The People of the Sierra*, 1954, a story of the social structure of a typical southern *pueblo*:

Courting takes place traditionally in Andalusia, at the reja (the grill which covers every window) and sentimental numbers in the music-halls and the romantic postcards sold on news-stalls portray a 'novio' so ardent that only iron bars can safeguard the purity of his love.

Courting traditions may have changed, but fortunately the lattice grilles remain, their delicately forged shapes a continued reminder of old customs and traditional skills. With new architectural fashions in the eighteenth century, metal structures were replaced by small glass conservatories particularly popular in northern seaside towns such as La Coruña and San Sebastián, where complete apartment blocks overlooking the harbour front were encased in glass. These glazed galleries, known as *miradores acristalados*, allowed residents to admire the street or the ocean view while giving protection from the strong sea winds.

The customs which guided the construction and

Early fortified castles were built with narrow window slits for defence. Later, in many popular rustic houses a top-floor balcony acted as a patio where the householders could sit out and take a few minutes of sun during the day. Walls both inside and out are generally whitewashed, but exterior walls painted with calsimined colours are common. The window balconies of grander establishments assume a more decorative, less convivial role.

Left The quirky decoration of fenestration often went to extreme lengths and patterns were painted onto exterior walls to give the appearance of added grandeur.

Below The Moors often built small windows facing the street in order to guard their privacy. Stained wooden shutters like these in Granada are a later addition but create the same secluded atmosphere.

Right Green louvred shutters surrounded by a mass of ivy are another means of decorating a façade whilst diffusing light and heat.

decoration of windows varied of course from one region to another according to climate, but there were underlying principles. Windows had to allow light to enter the room and at the same time keep heat and cold out. Wooden shutters and external slatted blinds were devised to fulfill that function. The shutter often had a hinged panel within it to reduce the size of the opening. Hinges were traditionally very simple and inconspicuous in their design; where elaborate strap hinges do exist, they bespeak French influence.

In high summer, when midday temperatures soar, shutters are kept closed during the day to prevent the heat from entering and circulating through a room. At night they are opened to clear any stuffiness and allow the soft scents of jasmine and Dama de la Noche to fill the air with their sweetness. It is common to find these plants, especially in the hotter climes of the south where they grow best, trained up the wall near to windows as their scent, so delectable to the human senses, is repellent to insects, especially mosquitoes.

Curtains gained popularity in Spain during the nineteenth century, but thick embroideries and tapestries were used long before then to cover walls and windows in the larger palaces of the north where insulation was a constant problem during long winters. Embroidered silk netting, on the other hand, was frequently used to diminish and diffuse the light.

Window seats, decorated with tiles and built into the overall structure of the wall, are another commonly adopted feature. They allow occupations such as needlework to be carried out under natural daylight, within the privacy and coolness of an interior room.

Exterior windows were often built high up, just under the eaves of the roof, so all invading light was diffused softly across the walls with a resonant dimness. So much natural light exists in Spain that its intensity must be controlled and the structural development of the window has always been checked by this one basic provision. This is often the case with *ajimez* windows, the distinctive double arched horseshoe windows divided by a column, which lend such sensitivity to the exceptional Mozarabic churches of Asturias and have remained popular to this day in both secular and ecclesiastical buildings. Their narrow, divided form diffuses light with sublime vehemence so sunshine enters an enclosure in dazzling beams only to be cut short by the wall and thence scattered like warm rain throughout the surrounding space.

123

124

Right The strange corner balconies, which add such distinction to the grand Renaissance palaces of Trujillo, are often adorned with richly sculpted masonry, in this case the arms of the Duques de San Carlos, founders of the Palacio de Vargas Carvajal.

Left Late-nineteenth-century apartment blocks in Valencia show the fanciful inclinations of local architects. A strong sense of Baroque exuberance remained a strong characteristic of domestic architecture in Valencia well after its popularity had diminished elsewhere in Spain.

126

There appear to be no rules whatsoever as to the shape and frame of Spanish windows, although exterior windows are on the whole smaller than those facing onto an interior patio.

Doors

In a similar way the Spanish door has always been regarded as having both a symbolic and practical importance, rooted in the Spanish love for extravagance. Keys were often painted into the face of Hispano-Moresque pottery to signify paradise and, if ever a sacristan is disturbed to open a church at an odd time of day for a passing traveller, he will, more often than not, have a bunch of oversized keys with which to accomplish the relatively easy task of springing the latch. On display in the chapter room of Seville's cathedral are the votive keys presented by the defeated Moors to King Ferdinand the Saint when he forced the complete surrender of the city to Christian dominion in 1248. Key-swapping, it would seem, was an accepted diplomatic practice between Christian and Arab rulers.

As important as this show of hospitality towards enemies was the elaboration of doors to reflect something of the reception to be expected within. The distinctive 'Hand of Fatima', which so serenely extends from the centre of many front doors, as if waiting for a kiss, once denoted Islamic sympathy, while the painting of doors in bright welcoming colours echoes the genial Spanish modus vivendi.

In contrast are the key-stone doors of Renaissance palaces in Extremaduran cities like Cáceres and Trujillo, which could comfortably be incorporated into the façade of a cathedral. These granite palaces were exchanged for the fortunes gained in the Americas and the dimensions of the entrances are generally out of all proportion to the windows. In their daunting gravity all the bold paranoia and merciless invincibility of the conquistadors is mirrored.

But size was generally related to practicality. The height and girth, in days past, had to accommodate horse, rider and carriage. For this reason many gates had a smaller rectangular portal, or *postigo*, built into them for pedestrian access.

Some of the most spectacular doors were built during the years of reconquest when Romanesque architecture prevailed. The Pórtico de la Gloria, where pilgrims entered the cathedral and shrine of St James at Santiago de Compostela, is widely considered to be the most exceptional decorative doorway in existence. Romanesque entrances, and the finely worked tympanums which crown many of them, were an exterior reflection of biblical teachings and survive to this day alongside the religious metaphors, grotesques and symbolism which dominated the Christian consciousness of the age. Gothic portals were generally more elevated but no

In the embellishment of doorways the Spanish imagination is no less inventive. The monolithic Plateresque entrance to the Palacio del Infantado at Guadalajara (right) is in complete contrast to the interior portal in the Alhambra (left), sumptuously surrounded with stucco carving, or to a simple pointed Gothic arch and wooden door in Catalonia (above).

130 In the first instance the door had to fulfil a basic function of security, whether it gave access to a vast Renaissance building like the Hospital de Tavera, an urban palace, a Romanesque church, or a town house.

With the rise of powerful local families in the fifteenth and sixteenth centuries, the ancestral escutcheon was inevitably incorporated somewhere into the composition, often above the keystone, so as to indicate the household's place and position. Status, or the aspirations of the owner, were often reflected by the doorway to a building; even the locks were given a sense of grandeur.

132

Stone architraves offered end-less possibilities for architects to explore their most excessive whims, reinterpreting line and form in often highly decadent ways.

134

less descriptive or sculptural, while those of the Renaissance emulated the more wordly concepts of nationhood; family escutcheons were lavishly carved above any portal worth its weight.

Arab and Mudéjar doors found greatest effect when married with the keyhole arched entrance. They were often hinged on the outside of the wall with the front swinging on pivots built into the stone sockets of the foundation. The Puerta del Perdón in the great mosque at Córdoba, plated with bronze and copper, is perhaps the finest example of all, with Christian heraldry and Gothic inscriptions richly intermixed with arabesques.

The Moorish door was constructed with the same fine mosaic of interlacing wooden geometries which so characterized the Mudéjar coffered ceilings. The finished surface of concentric rectangular planes lent itself directly to lavish metal decoration, unlike Gothic doors which were generally hewn with all the skill possessed by the carvers of the day.

Door hardware in Spain developed in a completely original way that was distinct from all other European styles, and comprises one of the most unique areas of Spanish decorative inventiveness. It is above all typified by the decorated nailhead, which quickly outgrew its practical function during the Middle Ages and became a typical ornamental fixture. As a reinforcement it lent an illusion of indestructability and yet the delicate workings of the

Left The great Baroque door to the palace of Alfabia, once the residence of the Moorish governor of Mallorca, was stripped of its bronze decoration and 365 nailheads in a local uprising in the last century.

Right The more flamboyant face of Spanish architecture is also manifested in its doorways. Here, it is the chimeric quality of surrounding stucco work that demands attention rather than the underlying structure.

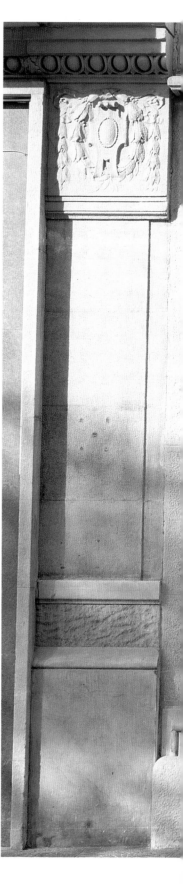

138

Door hardware progressed to a decorative extreme as bosses, hasps, knockers, backplates, hinges and key holes were stamped, incised and fashioned into the most imaginative shapes. The most irrational applications of all can still be seen on the thirteenth-century doors leading into the Cistercian church at Meira in Galicia (far right).

140

oversized nailheads gave exuberant grace and balance to the overall design of the door. Nailheads could take on any disguise. They often adopted the shape of scallop shells, flower motifs and convex bosses while fine engraving invested them with a deeper mystery.

Of equal ornamental importance was the door knocker or *llamador*, which metamorphosed into lizards, reptiles and imaginary figures lurking in the Gothic imagination. The practice spread into the embellishment of hasps, hinges, keyholes, locks and lockplates, all of which were worked with similar delicate ingenuity and remained in production until the eighteenth century. They were then replaced by *aldabas*, decorative iron rings with backplates, which became the most common type of knocker to be seen on palace doors throughout Spain. Often-forged into spiral shapes and incised with floral patterns in an equally intricate manner, they demonstrate the continuing skills of the Spanish smiths.

To this day the embellishment of windows and doors continues to be an external expression of a household. The general austerity of the Spanish façade found release through their adornment: to the stranger they act like a keyhole into the interior.

Far left The Hand of Fatima on a door generally indicated Moorish occupation. Examples of this evocative image survive from the thirteenth century, although this example is much later.

Left A typical Andalucian back street complete with a *tejaroz*, the little roof above a doorway.

Right and below In a country where so much life exists on the street, the door remains the link between the private and public life of the household.

Below right Two lizard-like dragons, a popular motif for door decoration in the sixteenth century, announce the arrival of visitors to this Spanish household.

INTERIORS

Spanish interiors

reflect the influence of two separate civilizations:

Arab and Christian. The Moslems instilled their homes with

a sense of comfort, contemplation and rich decoration, often wildly decadent.

The Christian home, by comparison, was generally more austere.

In the mingling of these two mentalities,

a number of hybrid styles

have emerged.

Left The games room shows the grand style in which the Pazo de Oca was remodelled in the eighteenth century.

Below The old kitchen, now a private sitting-room, retains many original features.

Right An ancestral portrait of three sisters hangs in the main *salon*, its walls draped with red damask.

Pazo de Oca

A Galician **M**anor **H**ouse

In the emerald green interior of Galicia, surrounded by the lands of the river Ulla where haystacks dot the fields like teepees, rise the Baroque belfries of the private chapel beside one of Galicia's most prestigious private homes – the Pazo de Oca. During the seventeenth and eighteenth centuries, the term *pazo* came to signify a country palace, similar to the English manor house, which acted as a catalyst for local rural life. It was more than just a retreat for the local gentry; it formed a vital part in the political, economic and cultural structure of the Gallegan community. The nobility of Galicia, unlike their equals in Castile and Aragón, did not abandon their ancestral castles for new Renaissance town palaces but instead turned them into farm estates which they would visit during the summer until the harvest was complete.

It is possible that the foundations of the Pazo de Oca were erected upon the remains of a twelfth-century fort, but the earliest part still standing is the square tower of the *casa fuerte*, or fortified house, constructed by the *pazo*'s founder, Don Suero de Oca. The main body of the house encloses a large, inner quadrangle of formal garden with a clover leaf-shaped fountain at its centre, and dates to the decades before and after 1700.

The garden encircling the Pazo de Oca is the oldest and most famous in the region. Two streams, the Boó and Mao, running through the property feed the numerous little *huertas* with fresh water. The avenues of towering lime trees and clipped hedges enclose, and open out upon, small orchards of apples, pears and lemons. Further out, beyond the glades of eucalyptus and pine, lie meadows and pastureland for the cows and sheep and neatly trellised vineyards.

The use of large blocks of local granite throughout the grounds for both practical and aesthetic purposes reaches a sculptural crescendo on the upper and lower lakes, representing heaven and hell, where the balustraded bridge and stone balls create extraordinary perspectives. In the 1920s, nineteenth-century romantic intrusions like the Swiss

chalet were eliminated, and its Baroque origins re-established.

Architecturally, the *pazo* is exceptional for such details as the porticoed galleries and the square coronet-like heads on the chimneys and is a good insight into the day-to-day functioning of a Spanish estate three hundred years ago. Almost all of the ground floor was given over to the needs of the farmworkers and the domestic necessities of the household: staff kitchens, pantries, carpentry shops, a small *bodega* where the 'house' wine fermented in large oak vats, a bakery, weaving room and plenty of drying space for the fruits, herbs, nuts, potatoes, maize, hams and sausages. These large storage areas were required as the *pazo* received all its rent from neighbouring tenant-farms in kind.

From the main entrance hall a staircase ascends to the residential quarters where major renovation works were undertaken in the late 1930s under the guidance of the last Marqués de Camarasa who did much to restore the original character of the *pazo*. On his death Oca passed to his niece whose father was the 17th Duque de Medinaceli. The estate is now part of the Fundación Casa Ducal de Medinaceli which maintains and restores all the family properties, including the Hospital de Tavera in Toledo and the Casa de Pilato in Seville. The foundation was established by the present Duque de Segorbe. His lasting achievement at the Pazo de Oca has been to restore the gracious equilibrium between the house, garden and estate.

146

A*bove left* A corner of the library is left as a testimony to the last Marqués de Camarasa.

A*bove and left* The principal staircase is shaded with linen sun blinds, woven in the *pazo*'s workrooms and incorporating a family crest of three trout.

R*ight* The Bedroom of the Three Sisters, whose portrait appears in the *salon*.

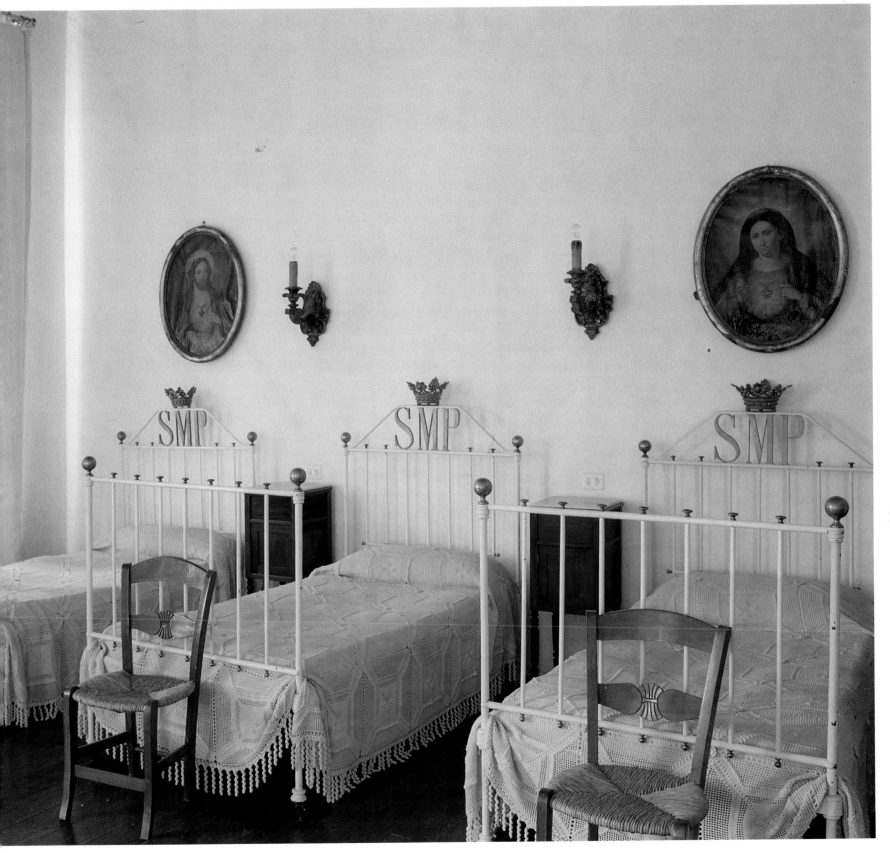

Casa del Marqués de Salvatierra

An Andalucian Town Palace

In 1485 the Salvatierra family, on account of the bravery and loyalty shown towards the Catholic monarchs during the week-long siege of Ronda, were granted estates and a house in the newly conquered town as part of the *repartimiento*, or division, of the territories. The senorial home which they subsequently built was, in line with the Renaissance traditions of the day, on the scale of a palace and it has remained in the family ever since.

For that reason it is a very strange phenomenon, for few palaces can claim such a pure, uninterrupted lineage. In every town in Spain there exist rambling señorial houses of a similar kind but hundreds of them lie empty and ruined or restored in a way which has little bearing with their ancestral past.

The Casa del Marqués de Salvatierra is a well-preserved showpiece of Spanish noble life as conducted through the last five centuries.

Part of the reason for the survival of the house must be attributed to the role the family has played in the Real Maestranza de Caballería de Ronda, a local noble brotherhood established in 1573 by Philip II to defend Ronda and the *serranía* from possible attacks from Moors and bandits, as well as to maintain and uphold such chivalrous arts as horseriding. Of the four other Maestranzas of Seville, Granada, Valencia and Zaragoza, none are as important as that of Ronda which is the oldest. In the Casa del Marqués de Salvatierra many of their meetings took place.

The walls in the garden are the only vestiges of the Moorish house which once stood on the site, ruled over by the sultan Abu Nur. Otherwise the con-

148

Top The imposing Mannerist façade of the palace, its fluted Corinthian columns supporting a wrought-iron balcony. The Inca figures serve as corbels and are symbolic of Ronda's prosperous association with the Americas.

Above A small ivory Christ in the private chapel was found buried in the garden after the Civil War. It has since been restored to its former Baroque splendour.

Left The drawing-room was redecorated in the nineteenth century with mahogany furniture and a 'cornucopia' mirror.

The entrance hall. Anonymous paintings of Philip IV and Mariana of Austria hang either side of a nineteenth-century heraldic drape. The *media naranja* ceiling implies the possible existence of an *artesonado* before the front part of the house was destroyed by fire in the early 1700s.

149

struction is almost completely original to the early sixteenth century while the interior dates to the period of major reform in the middle of the eighteenth century. This was a particularly prosperous time for the people of Ronda who built a bridge across the great limestone chasm, El Tajo, gouged out by the river Guadalvin in order to connect the new town with the old Moorish neighbourhood.

The Salvatierra family were more closely connected with a project for the building of the new bullring, the largest in Spain and arguably the most beautiful. Every September the people of Ronda and the Maestranza gather to take part in the *corrida goyesca*, the Goya bullfight, when ticket-holders dress in the traditional costumes of the eighteenth century and celebrate the era of Francisco Romero, who is credited with the invention of bullfighting on foot and whose skills were captured so fluently by the freehand sketches of Goya in his Tauromaquia series.

The Casa del Marqués de Salvatierra is a tribute to the determination of the family who have withstood the tribulations of Spain's long and frequently tempestuous history and preserved with such care a unique piece of Spain's heritage.

Far *left above* Copper-coloured
vine leaves create an autumnal
roof for a courtyard, supported
by fluted stone columns
wrapped in the slithery coils of
carved mythic beasts. The stone
slab floor is inset with patterned
tiles for decoration.

Far *left below* A view across the
ancient Moorish battlements,
encrusted with creepers,
towards the distant Serranía de
Ronda.

151

L*eft* Terraced gardens are given
an air of formality with closely
clipped evergreen parterres and
fanciful topiary. Walls are
painted in bright yellow-ochre
hues, which contrast with the
luxuriant foliage.

Palacio de Caravia

An Asturian Country Palace

It is difficult to envisage that in 1971 this exquisite example of a late Renaissance palace of northern Spain was moved, pillar by pillar and stone by stone, from the heart of the old fishing port of Ribadesella, poised at the estuary of the river Sella, to a magnificent and isolated hill-top a few miles inland from the cliff-strewn coast of Asturias.

In the process of transference nothing was overlooked and the character of the property was immaculately preserved down to the last detail. It was an endeavour which required both a certain courage upon the part of the owner and a complete understanding of local architectural traditions by those employed to reconstruct the palace on new foundations.

Even in its former situation, the Palacio de Caravia was considered one of the most important palaces of Asturias. The building possessed in its simplicity all the architectural purity and delicate grandeur of the unique ninth-century Asturian churches, which served as royal residences for the early Asturian kings, who initiated the reconquest and kept alight the embers of Christianity in a land overrun by Islamic culture.

The palace dates from 1700, a period when Renaissance fashions were still alive in Asturias. The strong classical proportions combined with the general lack of exterior decorative ostentation – except for the family coat-of-arms – and the large blocks of stone are all typical of a much earlier period encountered elsewhere in Spain.

Many of these forms did not reach the deeper recesses of the country until a much later date, where they remained a potent force. But there are some features which are clearly characteristic of northern Spanish architecture. The wood and glazed gallery running along the first floor of the palace, thereby creating a beamed roof for a ground level portico, is typical of the area where the interior patio is a rare phenomenon. Similarly, the elegant stone arched causeway connecting the house with the small private chapel is another graceful peculiarity rarely seen in the south.

In the choice of the new site many factors were taken into consideration, but the most important was unquestionably the vista. The windows of the Palacio de Caravia look south towards the mighty peaks of the Picos de Europa, which for centuries were a vital navigational landmark for ships sailing up and down the coast and now form one of the country's most important national parks. To the north, the great blurred horizon of the Atlantic is visible. It is a unique prospect and when standing in the garden it is almost impossible to believe the Palacio de Caravia was ever anywhere else but here.

Far *left* The Palacio de Caravia with its family coat-of-arms, typical of senorial Spanish residences.

Left A seventeenth-century fountain and classical statues guide the eye towards the magnificent view south to the Picos de Europa, one of the last refuges of the European brown bear.

Above The main *salon*, which runs the full length of the gallery, speaks clearly of the palace's former site in Ribadesella – an important fishing harbour: a masted schooner sits on the mantlepiece and an old maritime map of Spain hangs above.

Right Private chapels are a common feature of large houses in Spain. The magnificent carved and gilded Baroque altarpiece in the chapel at Caravia has largely escaped the bright brush of the eighteenth-century polychrome painter.

Hospital de San Juan Bautista

The Private Apartments of the Dukes of Medinaceli

The Hospital de San Juan Bautista (or St John the Baptist), also known as the Hospital de Tavera, faces the gate of Bisagra just outside the old perimeter walls of Toledo. The rusticated stone walls contain a monastery and apartment rooms divided by the chapel from a hospital and a vast subterranean crypt – the pantheon of the Duques de Medinaceli and Lerma. This massive and imposing building predates the royal monastery of El Escorial and shows early indications of the later Herreran Renaissance style.

In 1541, the philanthropic Cardinal Tavera ordered his secretary, Bartolomé de Bustamente, to draw up plans for a charitable institution to serve as a hospital for the people of Toledo. Bustamente had spent a great part of his early life travelling through Italy and in the Hospital of San Juan Bautista he faithfully copied the forms and proportions of the Italian High Renaissance. Much of the work was carried out by Alonso de Covarrubias, one of Castile's greatest Renaissance architects.

The apartment rooms were restored earlier this century by the Duquesa de Lerma as a faithful representation of a sixteenth-century Spanish interior. It is not easy to define exactly the Spanish Renaissance interior. There are no records and all palaces of that age have at some stage fallen on hard times, their subsequent restoration carried out with respect to later fashions. However, the Duquesa de Lerma's interpretation is undoubtedly the most authentic example of the grand senorial taste of the Spanish Renaissance.

Walls were always whitewashed and hung from ceiling to floor with Flemish tapestries. Decoration was kept simple apart from the chimney and wainscot. Furniture was heavy and placed against the wall apart from tables running down the centre. Rooms were large, tall and airy, the windows set back and generally diminutive or covered with wooden latticed shutters.

The reconstructed apartment rooms in the Hospital spread across the south-west wing and look up towards the mass of tiled roof tops and Mudéjar towers of the ancient Visigothic capital. Apart from the dining-room, the ground floor is taken up almost entirely by the library. Many of the books date back to the period when Toledo contained the leading translation schools west of Byzantium during the thirteenth and fourteenth centuries.

The severity of white walls in these large stately

The courtyard of the Hospital de San Juan Bautista is made up of 96 arches and 112 columns on two levels – Doric below and Ionic above – with a unique, two-storey gallery dividing the court down the middle. The architect, Bartolomé de Bustamente, conceived this on a larger scale than any he had seen during his Italian travels.

155

rooms is broken not only by rich hangings but also by a magnificent collection of paintings including works by Ribera, Zurbarán, Tintoretto, Sánchez Coello and Caravaggio. Several works are by El Greco, who lived in a house on the far side of the city and was commissioned on occasions by the Hospital. Here, some of his most important paintings can still be appreciated in their intended settings, including the *Baptism of Christ* and *The Tears of Saint Peter*. El Greco died whilst working on a commission here.

From the library a staircase leads up to the next floor, which has a large room for entertaining and off it a bedroom, joined to a smaller, more private sitting-room. Again the atmosphere of the age is effectively recreated with heavy oak furniture, *bargueños* and chests. The original wainscot runs around almost every wall and is made of patterned Talavera pieces running above and below a row of baked terracotta tiles.

Through its long history the Hospital has been used as an orphanage, monastery, school and exhibition centre but its sheer scale has never ceased to express the original Renaissance intentions of its founder. Presently it is undergoing general renovation works under the guidance of the Fundación Casa Ducal de Medinaceli.

Above The Hospital de San Juan Bautista possessed one of the most important pharmacies in Castile. A painted cupboard was used to store recipes which included such ingredients as herbs, spices and precious stones. The pharmacy also served as the dispensary, with its measures, scales, giant pestles and a special box containing phials of different poisons.

Left The dining-room, with a vast portrait of Charles V by Titian and a portrait of the founder, Cardinal Tavera, above the fireplace. Most of the stone carving in the Hospital, including the cantilevered fireplace, is by Alonso de Berruguete. The red velvet-covered chairs and wrought-iron chandelier are typical of sixteenth-century Spanish interiors.

The bedroom is austerely furnished, but the four-poster bed is a sumptuous affair: green velvet drapery is embroidered with gold thread, delicate ironwork is fashioned into decorative finials, as well as an ornate chandelier. An ivory Christ hangs above the bed; religious imagery remains a prevalent feature of Spanish life.

157

Casa de la Lama

A Senorial **M**ansion **H**ouse in **S**egovia

Beneath a cascade of jasmine and ivy, the last arch of the massive Roman aqueduct in Segovia is to be found behind the walls of the Casa de la Lama. It is a peculiar garden folly which suggests that a house has existed on this site since the days of the empire of Trajan. In recent years the gardener has solved part of the mystery by digging up fragments of a Romanesque capital and an exceptional frieze depicting a mermaid lounging on a rock.

The house is typical of the area and is built about a colonnaded courtyard with a granite fountain at its centre. The lower rooms originally served as stables but are now used as utility rooms. A wooden staircase capped by a seventeenth-century *artesonado* ceiling ascends to the first floor where the main rooms of the house are to be found, leading off a glassed-in gallery with old scrubbed plank floors, both typical features of the Castilian interior.

The palace has belonged to the Cabanyes family for several generations and is a testament to their Catalan roots which have produced a line of artillery officers, knights of Calatrava and architects, as well as the Romantic poet Manuel de Cabanyes, the Spanish Keats, who died of tuberculosis at the age of twenty-six on the same day his first volume of poetry was published.

The Romantic movement spread throughout Spain in the middle decades of the nineteenth century, and the rooms still echo with the sentimental serenity of those times. The house is a perfect period example of a nineteenth-century Isabelline interior. The conduct of the Segovian nobility was such that the main *salones* were only used when the monarch visited. Since this happened infrequently they remain almost unchanged, if a little jaded.

Major restoration works to the house were undertaken by Crisilda de Vivanco in 1870, which complied very much with the interior expected of polite provincial society. The stained glass front to the small chapel and the frieze of *scagliola* around the galleries and in the guest bedrooms were both popular forms of decoration and are to be seen in many similar palaces of the era.

The dining-room, drawing-room and main bedroom run along the southern façade of the house overlooking the aqueduct. On the top floor a studio has replaced the old servants' quarters. Few modern encumbrances spoil the authentic period atmosphere of the house where a becalmed tranquillity prevails.

158

Right The delicate colours of the gallery walls have softened from years of exposure to the strong Castilian light, which is only partially diffused by the Belgian scalloped-lace blinds.

Left In the latter part of the nineteenth century the size of rooms was reduced in line with French fashions, and the desire for comfort expressed through the introduction of pieces of furniture like the day bed. The pale gold colours and fabrics of this *salon* are a subtle interpretation of the taste of Segovian society. The wallpaper is original to when the house was last redecorated in 1895.

Below The cantilevered staircase is made from pine, imported from Northern Europe as the local variety is too soft for such purposes.

Left Romantic fever spread throughout Spain in the middle decades of the nineteenth century. The main bedroom, with its rich red furnishings and delicately fashioned, brass-canopied bed, is lit by a cut-glass chandelier from the royal glass factory at La Granja.

159

The upper storey gallery surrounding the main rooms of the Casa de Pilato. A diary written by the poet Juan de Encina, who accompanied Don Fadrique, 1st Marqués de Tarifa, on his long pilgrimage through Italy to the Holy Land, relates vividly the magnificent buildings they encountered along their journey, which had an undoubted effect on the plans for the house.

160

La Casa de Pilato

A Sevillian Palace

It remains a tradition in Seville for the robed and hooded Confraternities in the Holy Week penitential processions to begin their *pasos* from a small plaza on the edge of the Barrio Santa Cruz. A small cross of coloured marble in the wall of the Casa de Pilato still marks the place where the Semana Santa processions begin. The route to Campo de Cruz along narrow, whitewashed streets is equal in length to the road walked by Christ on his way to Golgotha.

When the 1st Marqués de Tarifa, Don Fadrique de Ribera, returned from his pilgrimage to Jerusalem in 1520, he built himself a sumptuous palace on the edge of the city. Gossip quickly circulated among the citizens claiming the plans were copies of those used for the Praetorium where Christ was sentenced. The new property was referred to as the Casa de Pilato – the house of Pontius Pilate, a title which became official in the nineteenth century.

The myths alone invest the house with an anomalous aura, but of a deeper importance are the characteristics which make the Casa de Pilato a living architectural legend. Early Gothic, Plateresque and Mudéjar elements harmonize sublimely. The pervasive atmosphere surrounding courtyards, galleries, public rooms and gardens alike is in the same instant lavishly Moorish and also magnificently Renaissance. From 1534 to 1539 carpenters, painters and glaziers were commissioned from Genoa to work with Seville's own artisans. No private building in Spain captures so perfectly the interaction of Islamic and Renaissance art forms.

Don Fadrique died in 1539 leaving two illegitimate daughters and no direct heir. The house passed to his cousin Per Afán Ribera III, Viceroy of Naples, a position which enabled him to fill Pilato with many important classical antiquities. The collection he amassed was that of a truly Renaissance spirit and included rare manuscripts, exceptional Greek statues, and marble busts built into niches around the courtyard. Two loggias were built about the patios to display his fabulous artefacts.

Under the 3rd Duque del Alcalá, in imitation of the Medicis, the house became a favourite setting for humanist *tertulias* where doctors, writers and artists would meet to discuss current ideas on medicine, politics and philosophy. But in the eighteenth and nineteenth centuries travellers such as the Italian Norbert Caimo wrote about the lamentable state of the palace which had fallen into ruin.

161

A detail of the main courtyard showing the marble pilasters and Plateresque masonry which are so typical of the many Moorish palaces of Spain. The columns vary in workmanship between courtyards due to restoration work carried out over the centuries, which also explains the uninterpretable cufic stucco rising vertical to the arch. Recent renovations revealed fragments of a mural which once extended around three-quarters of the courtyard. Painted between 1538 and 1539 by Andrés Martin, Alonso Hernández Jurado and Diego Rodríguez, it depicts Roman philosophers and orators.

Richard Ford in 1845 spoke of the 'scandalous state of neglect.' Romantic sensibilities came to the rescue and soon afterwards the careful restoration began in accordance with the original plans which still exist.

The mere titles of the great rooms conjure up images of the illustrious past of the palace: the Withdrawing Room of the Judges; Pilate's Reception Room; the Antechamber to the Chapel; the Fountain Room. Each room, with its *artesonado* ceiling, is uniquely decorated with hangings, paintings, objects and furniture.

The staircase and ground-floor rooms are no less remarkable for the fully tiled dados, pulsating with colours and arabesques, many stamped with the *escudos* of the Ribera and Mendoza families. This is where the full Mudéjar influence is discovered.

Water channels lead out to two gardens. The area to the south is extensively tiled and adorned with benches, sculptures and lily ponds. Swallows dive through the warm air skimming the limpid surfaces. To the north, the patio is green and the beds, laid with different coloured earths, are quartered about a fountain with foot paths running alongside the tranquil shaded avenues of plants, trees and black-stemmed bamboo.

The house, which remains the main residence of the present Duquesa de Medinaceli, perfectly describes the influence of lingering Moslem culture upon prevailing Renaissance taste.

Above left Gilded Mudéjar woodwork is displayed on the sixteenth-century coffered ceiling. The bas-reliefs and coats-of-arms are two of the most common features which distinguish this utterly Spanish form.

Above A turned walnut table and chairs are positioned beneath a dark painting of the Sevillian school.

163

Left A view of one of the principal *salones*. The roof is open to the ceiling and the exposed beams have been filleted with strips of rare wood. Interlacing stucco work surrounds the windows with a delicate ivory tracery and also acts as the cornice. Richly-coloured Eastern carpets cover the simple tiled floor.

164

Palacio de los Chaves-Mendoza

A Renaissance Palace in Extremadura

No private domain reflects more clearly the continuation of the Spanish love for decorative exuberance than the Palacio de los Chaves-Mendoza, facing onto the quiet little plaza in the old conquistador town of Trujillo, which rises from the granite wastelands of Extremadura. Behind the simple whitewashed façade and aggressive doors studded with star-shaped nail heads lies the country retreat of Duarte Pinto Coelho, whose taste, as he readily admits, is 'utterly Spanish ... flamboyant and touched with a little personal fantasy.'

The Chaveses were an important local family with a fortune created from the early colonization of Peru, which was conquered by another infamous dynasty from Trujillo, the Pizarros. The palace was probably built as an ancestral home for one of the offspring. In the eighteenth century the property was sold to nuns and converted into a convent at which point the chapel and courtyard were added. But Trujillo began to decline in the aftermath of the Napoleonic wars, when the palace was used to billet troops. Though the nuns somehow managed to struggle on, their fate was sealed by the dissolution of the monasteries in 1836. The palace fell into virtual ruin; but an American couple, Mr and Mrs Vanderbilt Whitney, came to its rescue, and hired Duarte Pinto Coelho to restore and redecorate the property with respect to its august origins. He later bought the palace for himself.

The great front doors open onto a typical arcaded stone patio whose grim arcades are vivified by blooming geraniums, ferns, orange trees, local antique furniture and unframed religious oil paintings, hanging high up on the walls. A vaulted first floor gallery looks out across this inner sanctum. The principal entrance hall is guarded by two dogs, one Spanish and fashioned in wood, the other French and made of terracotta. They wait patiently beside a seventeenth-century cardinal's bench. The expansive main rooms on the ground floor were created by knocking down several dividing walls to produce a sense of grandiloquent space. In the dining-room a barrel-vaulted ceiling was recreated by local builders using the ruins of a nearby house, and the nuns preference for tiles was replaced by slabs of local stone. The staircase to the first floor is a replica of the stairway in the Monastery of Guadalupe, made of red jasper, which led to the *camarin*, or dressing-room of the black Madonna. Upstairs the small cells of the palace have been opened up and

Far *left* In the canary-yellow breakfast room popular terra-cotta figures are ranged on the shelves above the fireplace. They were made in Malaga in the nineteenth century and represent typical figures of Andalucian life such as bull-fighters, gypsies, labourers and bandits. The watercolours of Spain are the work of Rossi, an Italian painter who travelled through Andalucia at that time.

Left The first-floor vaulted gallery runs around the four sides of the patio and is hung with seventeen naive portraits of Roman emperors, interpreted from Suetonius' *The Lives of the Caesars*. The hands are typical Spanish reliquaries and the chest was carved in Castile in the seventeenth century.

165

166

Above left In the private chapel the plaster, which once covered the columns in order to prevent the spread of plague, has been stripped away to reveal an authentic granite austerity, relieved by the rich red and gold hangings in traditional Spanish colours. The floor is of local slate.

Left In the dining-room the vaulting, known as *boveda de cānon* or barrel vaulting, was copied from a nearby ruin. The eighteenth-century English mahogany table is surrounded by Queen Anne-style chairs, found in the provincial capital of Cáceres. The imposing pictures on the wall are in the manner of Velázquez and depict Roman emperors on horseback. Exquisite Spanish metalwork is displayed in the form of candle sconces and Islamic-style lanterns.

L*eft* A typically eclectic corner of the house contains a portrait of an elector of Saxe-Coburg-Gotha, a polychromed statuette of a South American Indian child, a chair from the reign of Charles III and an Alcora urn, which stands upon an Indo-Portuguese embroidered cloth.

R*ight* The focal point of the main guest room is the nineteenth-century brass bed, topped by a coronet and smothered in lace drapery. A *petit-point* carpet depicts animals and floral designs.

R*ight* The patio of the Palacio de los Chaves-Mendoza, its arches wreathed in ivy, is an eight-eenth-century addition to the original palace. The well, with its delicate wrought-iron frame, was bought from a house in Sanlúcar de Barrameda and was installed during the restoration works carried out under the instruction of Duarte Pinto Coelho. Stone troughs overflow with scarlet geraniums.

167

turned into seventeen bright, informal and airy bedrooms.

Every inch of the palace is filled with the eccentric plunder of an insatiable collector: Napoleonic boxes; local woodwork such as bowls, carpentry tools, pestles and mortars; Spanish porcelain; and an exceptional collection of plates stacked up in the pantry. But any sense of clutter is negated by the commanding sense of space.

Lack of any particular style has allowed Churri-gueresque exuberance to co-exist with Renaissance majesty, and even popular vernacular designs typi-cal to Extremadura. What unites the palace is an overpowering feeling of ancestry, of an interior that has evolved over a very long time and is not simply the whimsical inclination of a single person.

L*eft* In the Goya Room the Stilt Dance is the most impressive of the tapestries. The royal factory in Madrid still produces designs by Goya on the original looms.

R*ight* Deeply carved pine doors lead into a guest bedroom, sparsely furnished, dark and cool. Decoration is provided by the inlaid bedhead, the red bedcover and Persian carpets.

Palacio de Viana

A Hispano-Moresque Palace

Tucked away on a quiet corner of the Plaza Don Gomé, in the crooked streets of the old bullfighters' quarter of Córdoba, stands the Palacio de Viana, a breathtaking example of a great Córdoban palace. The impressive carved stone entrance is embellished with the arms of the original owners, the Saavedra family, and records their long association with the order of the Golden Fleece. It opens into a large white arcaded courtyard filled with sculptural amphorae in wrought-iron stands from which sprout cactus plants. In the centre, a towering palm tree sways gently in the warm breeze, communicating to all who enter that this is another sanctuary of beauty and gracious living.

The conglomeration of rooms is unique and diverse, built about a succession of exquisitely maintained patios, fourteen in all, which fill the house with a thousand sensations of colour, shade and smell. The layout of the gardens dates from the tenth to the twelfth centuries when Córdoba flourished as the artistic capital of the western world, producing such notable scholars as Averroës and Maimonides. The house is of later origins and,

Left This is the most richly furnished *salon* in the palace, its seats upholstered with Flemish tapestries depicting mythical scenes. The large Solomonic columns were once part of a Churrigueresque altarpiece.

Below A frequently encountered Spanish setting: heavy, carved furniture with heraldic tapestry against a whitewashed wall. The traditional terracotta wainscot is edged with decorative ceramic tiles.

169

together with the garden, spreads across a surface area of over 6,500 square metres.

The number of foreign decorative influences which have been incorporated into the overall design of the interiors is of particular interest. On the ground floor the strong Flemish influence, which existed in Spain from the time of the great wool markets of Castile, can be seen in the numerous tapestries and the nineteenth-century chandeliers which hang from the ceiling of almost every room. A large gun cabinet contains important examples of arquebuses made by the royal gunsmiths and others from Flanders. The kitchen, however, is typical of southern Spain with sculptural alcoves that contain a collection of plates and kitchen bowls made in the pottery shops of Talavera de la Reina and Puente del Obispo.

On the second floor an encircling gallery of windows overlooks the patios, serving as space in which to hang the important collection of paintings of the Sevillian school. Rooms leading off it include a library of rare books on hunting; *salones* devoted to tapestries designed by Goya and from the French Gobelins factory; a dining-room with a chestnut coffered ceiling and exquisite examples of Alcora porcelain and locally made Córdoban leather; an anteroom comprised entirely of Portuguese Baroque furniture; and a rather despotic-looking bedroom furnished in a prevalently French style.

But the room which somehow typifies the Palacio de Viana is the room on the second floor where five allegorical paintings by Jan Brueghel are hung against the white walls. These imaginary interiors, depicted in infinitesimal detail, seem to capture the essence of the palace – a sensualist's paradise – where decorative resplendency spills out into the patios. Here, roses and jasmine entwine themselves around the trunks of ancient fig trees, their heady scent mingling with that of lavender and sweet basil; and the vivid colour of carnations and geraniums is tempered by the verdant foliage of myrtle and boxwood.

170

L*eft* A stone fountain plays at the centre of a small courtyard garden, surrounded by arched cloisters. The fan-shaped Roman mosaic that decorates the wall was transported from the Marqués de Viana's estate on the outskirts of Córdoba in the 1920s.

R*ight* The formal gardens again have water as their theme. Edged with soft grey-green spheres of centaurea, a central pool lined with ceramic tiles is punctuated by fountains which spout from lotus basins.

A*bove* Blue-painted shutters open onto wrought-iron balconies from which to enjoy the cool evening breezes.

171

La Viñuela

An Andalucian Country House

La Viñuela seems to hang above the world in the midst of a line of mountains to the left of the Guadalquivir basin in the area known as the Serranía de Ronda. For many centuries it was a wild and neglected part of Andalucia, forming a natural barrier between Seville, the sea and the kingdom of Granada. But the prospect has changed remarkably in recent times. The land has been tamed, the clay-tiled towers of Andalucian farmhouses, or *cortijos*, dot the fertile valley. The hillsides have been ploughed up and planted with undulating fields of sunflowers, while wheat fields and olive groves roll softly away towards the horizon.

The architect, Mario Connío, bought La Viñuela seventeen years ago from nuns in Ronda who were bequeathed the house by a rich local lady. She had built the house as a small country retreat where she could retire during the blazing heat of summer. What attracted him immediately were the dimensions – a perfect square, fourteen metres by fourteen, with a small inner courtyard.

From this simple classical core, Mario Connío set about enlarging the house with a series of extension wings added to each side. Through simple but ingenious tricks of perspective – large windows with infinite vistas of the landscape and double glass doors leading out onto pavilion-like terraces – he manipulated space and turned the humble cube into something altogether magnificent.

Each room emanates a sense of elegance and comfort, enhanced by personal possessions collected on various travels. Subtle colours reinforce the calm atmosphere; and custom-designed fireplaces punctuate the limited room space. In the winter when cold winds blow from the Sahara, the windows are shuttered, curtains block the draughts and scrub-oak logs crackle in every hearth.

The interior classicism continues into the garden where neat young orchards of almonds, citrus trees and figs, divided by pebbled pathways and lines of fountains, reach out towards the vast panoramas of the expansive *serranía*. The mind and eye cannot help but continuously gather the interior, garden and landscape into one coherent whole. The underlying Moorish influence of the garden combined with Mario Connío's original eye for colour, his deep understanding of architectonic form and an acute sense of interior movement make this house a personal but modern interpretation of the classical Andalucian country home.

Left Cypress trees are used to break up the panorama surrounding La Viñuela. In the spring the mountains of the Serranía de Ronda blaze with the colour of sunflowers and wild red poppies. A shallow moat surrounds this side of the house and, in Arabic fashion, effectively links house to garden.

Right Every room, even the bathroom, has a garden view that extends the perspectives of the house into the infinite distance.

173

Looking through into the main *salon*, which runs the full length of the front façade with fireplaces set into opposite corners. The curtains, which were found in Ronda, are made of old velvet, edged with a braid fringe. Plenty of Andalucian sunlight enters the room from two large doors that lead out into the garden. In the summer, outside blinds are drawn to block out the heat and all direct sun. The ceiling was frescoed by Mario Connío and his friends.

174

Left Varying shades of deep blue-green and sunshine yellow, typical of Andalucian farmhouses, are used in these guest bedrooms.

Right A view from the main entrance looking through the house and central courtyard to the other side. Patterned pebbles flank the cooling waters that pass through the courtyard, covered in summer with a white linen canopy to keep the house cool.

Above A pavilion-like terrace with a roof of trellised grapevines is joined to the house and used for dinner on summer nights when the landscape glimmers under the starlight.

Right The first-floor gallery, or *mirador*, stretches across the southern side of the house, a later extension to the villa built in the early nineteenth century. Cotton blinds are let down to filter the excess of southern light during the summer.

Below An upstairs bedroom with a mahogany Empire-style bed. English etchings hang either side of a velvet-framed mirror and the bookcase, with its leather-bound volumes, adds richness to the room.

Oceja

A Nineteenth-Century Summer Villa

The earliest summer resort towns in Spain were not, as one might have expected, on the Mediterranean but were built along the wide sandy beaches of the Atlantic coast around the small fishing villages of Cantabria. In the last half of the nineteenth century it was Comillas which became the most fashionable, mainly due to a certain Latin American shipping magnate and millionaire, Antonio López y López. He decided to make Comillas his new home after returning from South America with other rich *indianos*, those Spaniards who emigrated to the colonies but returned after independence.

Due to his generous acts of local philanthropy, López was finally made Marqués de Comillas, and a towering statue of him still stands on a promontory above the town, which ships from his transatlantic fleet used to salute whenever they passed by on their way to and from the industrial ports in the Bay of Biscay.

The Marqués bought for himself a large rectangular-shaped house on the edge of the village, which was most probably built in the early nineteenth century. In 1882, however, massive alterations were undertaken in readiness for the vacational visit of King Alfonso XII, who was to stay in Comillas as a guest of the Marqués. Quite naturally, the most progressive and fashionable architects of the time were commissioned from Barcelona to carry out the work, among them two of the most promising of the new emerging generation: Antoni Gaudí and Domènech i Muntaner.

The Villa Ocejo is a showcase for the more experimental forms of Modernist interior decoration, which were undoubtedly tempered by the patron's personal wishes but nevertheless bear close comparison to similar motifs and designs current elsewhere in Europe, especially England.

The incorporation of a large glassed-in gallery or *mirador* across one complete side of the house opened the main rooms onto the garden and the fresh Atlantic breeze; for most of the day the house is bathed in the warm southern light which can be regulated by the windows and white cotton blinds. The breakfast room on the east wing, which was most probably used as a conservatory during the winter, is infused with light in the morning. The Villa Oceja was built for a specific moment, a few languid summer days when the king came to visit. Fortunately it has remained exactly as it was originally conceived – a historical memento.

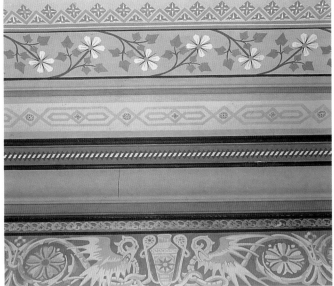

Above left The view of lush green grass and orange trees says something of the climate which made Comillas so popular as a summer resort with the Spanish nobility.

Above Layers of pattern on pattern create a sumptuous sensation in the Proustian Room. All around the room run hand-painted friezes of floral motifs or geometric designs.

177

Left The Proustian Room, decorated specifically for Alfonso XII, with cushioned cane furniture and fabric designs undoubtedly influenced by the work of William Morris. Only the chandeliers, bought in the Madrid flea market, El Rastro, are not typical of the period.

Left The Casa de Consell is found at the end of an old farm track within half-an-hour's drive of Mallorca's capital, Palma. It is surrounded by citrus orchards and olive groves.

Right The cottage is fed with fresh spring water from the original well on the staircase landing. It would once have been used for both animals and workers and still supplies cool, clear drinking water.

Casa de Consell

A Labourer's Cottage in Mallorca

The natural way of living for the Spanish has always been based upon the community. Unlike other countries in Europe there are surprisingly few country houses, and although isolated farmhouses like the Galician *pazo* or Andalucian *cortijo* do exist, the general tendency has always been for Spaniards to group themselves into villages.

It is no different on Mallorca, where most livelihoods depended, until the arrival of mass tourism, on the fruits of the earth and the sea, and there were hundreds of little hamlets dotted throughout the countryside and all along the coast. The only independent rural houses on the island were the *sones*, but even they were generally owned by absentee landowners who would visit their estates when the heat of the city grew too stifling.

In the summer, labourers were employed from the surrounding towns to help bring in the harvest, but as transport was slow and daily commuting impossible, the estates had to provide accommodation for the temporary workers. These houses were usually built in the very centre of the country, at the end of mule tracks, and constructed in a very basic manner. Casa de Consell was one such place and in its original state merely provided basic living requirements for the hired hands.

The structure was understandably simple. Downstairs was a large communal room for eating, playing cards and relaxing. The chimney for cooking and sink for washing were the only amenities provided by the employer. The upper floor was used as a large dormitory. A partition separated the men from the women and any extra space was used for storing the grain.

Many of these cottages have in recent years been converted by locals and foreigners into weekend cottages or simple holiday hideaways. Casa de Consell has belonged to a family from Palma de Mallorca for several years now and they have restored it in sympathy with the pure rusticity of the country's breathtaking landscape.

The basic structure is supported by wooden beams with limestone blocks around the windows and doors. The walls are made of local rubblestone, fixed with mortar and plastered and whitewashed inside so as to preserve the natural surface of the stone. Local wine bottles and decanters act as a decorative element in a corner of the kitchen. Mallorca has a long history of glass manufacture dating back to Carthaginian times – a deep blue hue is very characterisitic of the island. A staircase with a modern railing made by a local smith leads to the next floor. On the landing stand old earthenware water pitchers and chairs that were found in the house. Upstairs, basic bedrooms have been installed. Everywhere simple Mallorcan materials have been used which has helped preserve something of the original character.

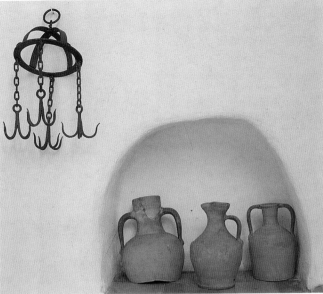

Above and right In the kitchen iron hooks, once used for hanging hams, sausages and game, are now used as decoration. The old stone sink is original to when the house was used by farm labourers.

Below To either side of a typical corner fireplace in the main living room are two rocking chairs covered in local Mallorcan fabric. Old three-legged milking stools serve as side tables.

179

Son Galcerán

A Mallorcan Country House

The term *son* is the general name ascribed to the ancient farm estates of Mallorca. These are grand houses, normally built in their own private valleys and surrounded by vineyards, olive groves, citrus orchards, gardens and farm buildings. Some date back to the age of the Moorish occupation of the Balearic Islands before James I reconquered Palma in 1229; others were built in a varying number of styles from the seventeenth century onwards, adopting architectural influences most typically from the villas of Tuscany. The *son* owners by tradition spent most of the time in their palaces in Palma or even Barcelona, only visiting their estates during the summer. For the rest of the year the *sones* were run by farm managers.

Sones, pronounced as in sonnet, are found throughout the island but many of the oldest examples, such as the Alfabia, the ancient country palace of the Moorish governors, are situated in the steep valleys of the inner foothills and along the coast of the Sierra de Trasmontana, the magnificent range of mountains stretching across the western side of the island from Sant Elm to the lighthouse at Cabo Formentor.

This steep and wild stretch of coast, navigable by one of the most beautiful country roads in Spain, was made highly fashionable during the nineteenth century by Luis Salvador Habsburg de Bourbon, known locally as the Archduke and one of the most eccentric characters of nineteenth-century Spanish society. A gentleman adventurer, he personified the spirit of the Romantic age. He fell in love with Mallorca as a young man and went on to create a form of alternative European court in exile, attracting about him important intellectuals, poets and artists. While other members of his family were busy scheming revolutions and extravagant suicides, the Archduke went off on expeditions to record the many varied botanical peculiarities of the island.

The Archduke set about restoring many *sones* for his friends and dependents, regenerating old gardens and introducing an international set to the ways of Mallorcan life. It was a lifestyle adopted later on by figures like Errol Flynn and Robert Graves. For his administrator, the Archduke built Son Galcerán on a promontory overlooking the sea near his own personal Son Moragues. Today it is the summer residence of Juan March, the grandson of the celebrated financier of the same name who rose from humble origins as a Mallorcan shepherd's son to

L*eft* The ivy loggia is illuminated on warm summer nights by iron and glass lanterns hanging from the red Mallorcan pine-beamed ceiling.

R*ight* Son Galcerán from the promenade running above the orchard.

F*ar right* Of all the rooms, the dining-room preserves the most authentic sense of the Archduke's era.

B*elow* A nineteenth-century copy of a Spanish Renaissance fireplace has been incorporated into the main drawing-room, with its modern, light colours. The nine paintings on the wall are part of a *mestizo* collection and depict the different genetic results of racial cross-breeding between the Spanish and the Indians of New Spain.

become one of this century's most celebrated international financial wizards and a great patron of Spanish art.

Son Galcerán was a present to Juan March from his father on his twenty-first birthday, but lay vacant until Juan decided to return to Mallorca and write a biography of the Archduke – a project which took him over seven years to research. It was while working on the book that restoration began.

Visitors to Son Galcerán are greeted by a cool entrance hall, tiled in a black and white chessboard pattern. The rooms on the ground floor retain their original nineteenth-century decoration with large shuttered windows looking across the farm orchards to the Mediterranean. A terracotta tiled terrace surrounds the house, which mixes the best of both European and Mallorcan taste. It provides a vantage point from which to enjoy the view.

On the top floor, Juan March's private apartments provide an escape into a Gatsby-like existence where he can work and write. During the summer he holds weekly *tertulias* which are always followed by grand parties. In the atmosphere of the entertaining rooms, Son Galcerán still reflects the age of the Archduke, who first introduced a highbrow cosmopolitan lifestyle to this idyllic island.

181

Casa de Carlos Sánchez Gomez

A Patio-House of Granada

The patio-house of Carlos Sánchez is situated in the heart of the old Nasrid quarter of Granada, in an area known as the Albaicín, a name which probably derives from the Arabic Rabadad el-Bayyazin meaning the 'place of the falconers'. Hidden away between crumbling old houses and narrow streets just wide enough for a mule to squeeze through, the house faces onto the Darro river, whose waters feed the fountains and pools of the Alhambra.

The house is built on a slightly sloping site and uses a rectangular groundplan built about three sides of an open patio. One wing rises to a height of two storeys while the opposite sides are on three floors. It was while renting an apartment in the house that Carlos Sánchez first noticed a number of features which seemed to indicate an important Moorish structure hidden behind years of replastering. In 1982 he bought the property and immediately began restoration work.

The first step was to uncover the original four-teenth-century elements which were still extant. As excavations proceeded, new features such as cobbled paving, the remains of horseshoe arches surrounded by richly carved stucco work, and parts of *artesonado* ceilings were brought to light. These elements were effortlessly incorporated into the new design with the result that the original character of a fourteenth-century patio-house has been perfectly recreated.

Traditional materials were used such as brick walls, timber floors and a roof made of clay roof tiles, while, as far as possible, the scale of each room was reconstructed with regard to the original Moorish structure. The house is a unique work of restoration which displays perfectly urban architecture

Above A collection of vivid blue glass from Castriz.

Left A fragment of the original *artesonado*, inlaid with boxwood and ivory, indicated enough to reconstruct this partially completed wooden ceiling. A Moroccan carpet is used for upholstery.

A wooden gallery, with light chamfered posts supported by double corbels, is typical of the patios of Granada. Orange trees planted to either side of the jade-green tiled pool add symmetry.

Right A triumvirate of horseshoe arches surrounded by richly carved stucco and marble tracery windows. All this work was done by local craftsmen using traditional methods and working from fragments of the original fourteenth-century Moorish design.

Below A common feature of Islamic domestic architecture is a small wall niche used for flowers or for burning incense. A doorway leads through from patio to house.

184

Far right The interior of the house continues to reflect the Moorish feel. Copper pots and Fajalauza bowls, manufactured by Moorish potters, sit on top of a typical oak chest. Eastern carpets used on wall and floor add to the richness.

185

in fourteenth-century Nasrid Granada. The transformation possesses all the exotic mystery of the Alhambra, albeit on a reduced scale.

The patio is of particular interest as it varies distinctly from those to be found anywhere else in Andalucia, and is typical of Granada. Its fundamental function, as a private and self-conceived setting in which to withdraw from the outside world, is emphasized by the orange trees and potted evergreen plants, and the square tiled pool with its attendant lotus fountain.

But what distinguishes the Granadan patio was the use of wood, and more specifically the construction of an upper gallery, or popular form of loggia. The probable reason for this was the fact that the Nasrid occupants of the house would have farmed part of the rich fertile *vega* surrounding Granada and would have used the gallery for practical purposes like drying fruits and corn, and keeping vegetables fresh. The wooden gallery remains a very common feature of popular Spanish architecture to this day and is still used for such purposes.

Castillo de Galiana

An Ancient Moorish Castle

From ancient records about the Visigothic capital of Toledo, it would seem likely that a building, founded by the great Bishop San Ildefonso, existed on the banks of the river Tagus on the road to Gaul. Whether this was a monastery or castle is hard to ascertain, but the probable position is the one occupied by the Castillo de Galiana.

The site could not be more perfect, with the garden meeting the bulrushes at the river's edge and the long view up across the fertile fields rising to the promontory where Toledo looms. From its privileged position, it lay utterly vulnerable, and was sacked by successive waves of invaders. With the routing of the Visigoths by the Arabs, stories of the castle move from obscurity into uncertainty.

It became the scene of a duel between a Christian and Moorish prince for the hand of a beautiful Arab princess who was later murdered by palace guards for her clandestine visits to feed captured Christian prisoners. Then nothing is known of the castle until Alfonso VIII refurbished it in a very oriental fashion for a Jewish temptress who had captured his heart. In 1525 Andrés Navagero, a wandering adventurer wrote: 'In this plain there is an old ruined palace which they call Galiana's. She was the daughter of a Moorish king who is the subject of many legends ... which are supposed to have taken place at the time of the Paladins in the court of Charlemagne ... the palace was a perfect place for such sagas.'

Ruined it remained until its impeccable restoration in the last few decades. Thin red bricks, so typical of Toledan Mudéjar architecture, have been used throughout for the walls, while *ajimez* windows allow the fresh breezes off the river into the rooms and out again across the *huerta* on the other side. The two large defensive towers have been converted into simple guest rooms which are used by family and friends in the summer. The surrounding grounds have been laid out with olive trees, cypresses, roses, herbs and shrubs typical of the dry gardens of Castile.

The castle is like a radiant romantic folly, set in a location from the *Rubaiyát of Omar Khayyam* with its open interior spaces joined by narrow passageways and winding staircases; its great olive jars standing steadfastly in the corners sprouting succulents and ivy; and the strong reflections in the sunken pond. The bright hovering patterns of dragonflies are all that disturb the green of the hedges, the red of the brick and the blue of the sky.

Left Large clay storage jars, once used for olives, wine or water, stand in every corner, sometimes planted with cacti or ivy.

Above In a deep-set alcove a large twenty-gallon wine bottle sits in its wrought-iron frame.

Right A view across the sunken garden to the main façade of the Castillo de Galiana. The castle is used mainly during the summer months.

The main hall downstairs is vaulted with red brick and is used for informal lunches during the summer. An *ajimez* window lets light and air into the room, which is exposed on the north and south sides to the garden.

Above Narrow passageways and staircases join the large spaces of the castle.

Above right A heavily studded doorway leads out into sun-filled gardens of terracotta pots filled with spiky yucca and cacti.

Right The top terrace, looking through a keyhole archway to one of the towers. From this vantage point, there are mag-nificent views across the *huerta del Rey* (the King's Orchard) and Toledo.

Far right Simple Spanish tables and benches are the basis of the furnishing of the castle.

Carmen de las Angustias

A Carmen in Granada

Of the many different types of Spanish house, the *carmenes* of Granada collectively possess a mystique and aura that places them in a category of their own. Half country-house and half urban-palace, they can be considered an early form of suburb in a very special setting – the shadow of the Alhambra. It was whilst staying in a *carmen* that St John of the Cross wrote some of his greatest metaphysical love poetry and, earlier this century, Manuel de Falla composed many of his most moving musical scores. Above all the *carmenes* are romantic houses where space is defined by the garden rather than the architectural structure, and the interior remains servile to the outside.

The Carmen de las Angustias in the heart of the Albaicín is a house which has been maintained both inside and out with a profound respect for the past. The main entrance is through an iron *reja* gate at the bottom of the garden, where a path ascends by way of a series of brick steps through avenues of trees and flowering pot plants to the front of the house.

From recent investigations, it appears that the whole house was rebuilt in the sixteenth century, but none of the original Moorish characteristics were retained, and it is quite probable that the site was destroyed during the siege of the Alhambra in 1491. The house is on three storeys, two above the street with a lower ground floor which leads through a portico directly into the garden. The main architectural innovation is a large shuttered glass gallery looking out across the tree-topped terraces. The rooms are long and narrow, and decorated in a way which reflects the wide and diverse taste of the present owner who has spent several years collecting objects typical of Nasrid Granada, as well as examples of fine Spanish iron work and intricate Mudéjar carpentry.

The interior extends out into the garden where a series of terraces have been planted with pears, hazelnuts, cypresses, magnolias, celindo, citrus trees, plums and peaches, all supplying plentiful shade. Ivy, jasmine and bougainvillea cover the walls like thick layers of bright paint.

The prevailing impression is of a very private inner city dwelling where garden and landscape are complemented by the interior – richly decorated galleries adorned with a collection of objects which complete the striking ambience of the Carmen de las Angustias.

Left In the dining-room a rare
carved Gothic panel of silhouet-
ted figures has been set into the
wall. The piece was probably
worked by Moorish carpenters
in Castile. The bench is a traditional piece of heavy Spanish
oak furniture and was probably
made in Medina de Rioseco,
near Valladolid.

Above Andalucia is strewn with
fragments of early terracotta and
pottery from the days of Roman
and Moorish occupation.

191

Far left A view from the marble-
columned portico to the garden
of the Carmen de las Angustias.
A fountain made from an old
church font forms a focal point,
surrounded by roses and a box
hedge.

Left Part of the large *salon* with nineteenth-century olive wood chairs made in Córdoba and a particularly important chest-of-drawers, used for monks' vestments and carved by Mudéjar artisans.

Below The square sixteenth-century *reja* in the colonnaded portico was taken from a monastery in Toledo. The stone, with its Visigothic-looking helix, was part of a door frame discovered in a ruined palace in Ubeda.

Right A typical Granadan fountain, with arched jets of water spurting into the basin below, is enclosed by clipped box hedges.

193

GARDENS

Courtyards and patios,

filled with fragrance and sunshine,

form a central axis for palaces and houses throughout Spain.

On hot languid days they act as peaceful sanctuaries where cascades of fragrant jasmine,

fulgent colours and the gentle sound of gurgling fountains

act as a balm upon the senses

and the garden becomes

a living extension

of the home.

The formal traditions of the Spanish garden derive from the Islamic belief in an earthly paradise. The garden should be a private retreat intended for relaxation; a place filled with shade and the soft murmur of fountains; with orchards of citrus fruit divided by pathways patterned with river pebbles, the breeze scented with jasmine and orange blossom; with brightly tiled courtyards paved with cool slabs of ivory-coloured marble and luxuriant climbing plants tumbling over the walls. In this setting, withdrawn from the outside world, the household and harem could gather for contemplation and pleasure. The earliest surviving examples of European garden design are directly inherited from the era of Arabic and Moorish rule and can be found in the patios and courtyards of Córdoba, Seville and Granada. The patio tradition has its variations from one city to another, from simple cloisters to grander arcades with lavish architectural detailing.

To the nomadic spirit the paradise garden, like an oasis, was a refuge. Shade and water were the most essential elements for repose after days spent in the desert, and once the itinerant tribes were settled in Spain, they began to appreciate its more sensual features. Abd al Rahman I, the first Caliph of Al-Andalus, was noted for his love of flowers. He sent emissaries to Turkestan and India to find the exotic plants that reminded him of the garden of his childhood. This was in the palace of Rusafa near Damascus, where he had lived before his family were driven out by the Abbasids. Roses, pomegranates and date palms came to Spain during his reign, and above all jasmine, which has remained one of the most widespread climbing plants of the Mediterranean.

The origins of the paradise garden are found in the Qur'an, which Moslems believe to be the Word of God dictated to Mohammed through the angel Gabriel. The Qur'an lays down rules as to how Moslems should live, and the garden, as a symbol of paradise, came to have paramount influence over every medium of Islamic art especially pottery, miniature painting and manuscript illumination. The design of the garden based upon rhythmic and geometric principles, is similar to the symmetrical weaves and patterns of an oriental carpet. The first gardens of this type were known as *chahar bagh*, or 'quartered gardens'; these were symbolically divided by four water channels which represented the four rivers of paradise, and emanated from a central fountain or pavilion, the whole enclosed by walls. As John Brookes wrote in *Gardens of Paradise*, 1987:

A*bove* The Alhambra, at the foot of the Sierra Nevada, has the idealized location of a romantic Arabian dream. A succession of courtyards, fountains and lily ponds are connected by walls carved with arabesques and shimmering tiled wainscots.

R*ight* The most magnificent Islamic patio in Spain is the Court of the Myrtles in the Nasrid Palace of the Alhambra in Granada. A dark algae grows profusely in the central pond to accentuate the reflection of the architecture in the still water.

L*eft* The fountain at the centre of the Court of Lions is supported by twelve beasts, each symbolizing a different sign of the zodiac. On their backs they support a heavily inscribed basin, representing the reservoir of the heavenly ocean.

197

The enclosed garden becomes a defined space, encompassing within itself a total reflection of the cosmos and, hence, paradise. Within it, this concept fosters order and harmony, and can be manifested to the senses through numbers, geometry, colour and, of course, materials. But the interaction of these elements of shape and space must create a place that is totally restful, devoid of tensions and conducive to contemplation.

The most evocative of these gardens stood within the grounds of the royal palace city of Medina az-Zahra, City of the Flower, built by Abd al Rahman III a few miles west of Córdoba. From the contemporary accounts by Moslem chroniclers, it must have been the most luxurious palace ever built; but sadly its splendour lasted only for a brief forty years. Excavation works are still in their earliest stages.

The ground plan occupied an area just under a square mile in size and was spread out across three terraces. At the top stood the distinctive horseshoe arches of the palace façade, while behind them stretched a succession of courtyards, entertaining chambers and royal apartment rooms with alabaster tracery windows looking out across the gardens.

198

Above The ascent to the Generalife winds across a ravine through an avenue of cypress trees to an outer garden, where hedges have been clipped to create tunnels and small shady glorietas, or arbours.

Left Marble lotus fountains gently murmur throughout the patios and gardens of the palace. Mohammed preached that a lotus-tree stands in the seventh heaven, to the right of the throne of God.

Right Nestling on a slope above the Alhambra is the Generalife (Garden of the Architect), the summer palace of the royal household. Arching sprays of water play across the central pool of the Court of the Canals, catching prisms of light in the late afternoon sun.

'He that hath two cakes of bread, let him exchange one of them for flowers since bread is food for the body but flowers are food for the soul' (Mohammed). Abu Zacarias's *Book on Agriculture* mentions the following flowers and herbs as being common to the Moorish garden – jasmine, roses, oleanders, arum lilies, irises, narcissae, mint, marjoram, lavender and thyme. Now, gardens are often filled with plants such as cock's comb, cone pepper, salvia and French marigold, many of which were introduced to Europe from Asia, Mexico and Brazil.

F*ar right below* The rose, introduced to Spain from Persia by Abd al Rahman I, was one of the most cultivated flowers in Islamic gardens and was charged with deep symbolism.

F*ar right above* Though flowers and their metaphysical meaning are central to Islamic art and imagery, the flower beds of the Alhambra are a very modern interpretation of how the garden was originally laid out.

Forming a central axis to these buildings was the Chamber of the Caliphs, entered by one of thirty-two doors carved from ivory and rock crystal and intricately damascened with gold, silver and bronze. The ceiling was forged from transparent slabs of marble which blocked out the heat and diffused the light. In the centre of the chamber stood a great fountain filled with mercury which dazzled and stupefied visiting Christian kings. Precious stones and metals were ransacked from throughout the Mediterranean and the far ends of the Islamic empire to decorate the interior. Over four thousand carved columns were used in the construction. The walls sparkled with emeralds and rubies set into the intricate stucco carvings and the floors were littered with cushions covered in richly embroidered silks.

201

The middle terrace was occupied by the main gardens, patios and orchards, where beds of purple violets released their soporific fragrance into the warm breeze. Peacocks, silver pheasants and birds with exotic plumage wandered freely in the shade, while lions were held in silver cages; gazelles ate windfall fruit and the golden carp in the ponds allegedly consumed twelve thousand loaves of bread each day. At night a thousand Nubian slaves dressed in gold and silver brocade lit the tiled pavilions with torches.

Right and left The Islamic garden was ideally evergreen, creating a feeling of eternal changelessness. Varying shades of green dominate the majority of Spanish gardens including those with more European origins.

Far left below and below Some of the most spectacular gardens of the Moors surround the sones of Mallorca – the farm estates of the Moorish nobility. Towering palm trees act as natural parasols and bamboo avenues create cool arbours over dappled cobblestone pathways, dampened by tiny jets of water.

Far left above The gardens of La Almudaina in Palma. James II built himself a garden menagerie in the grounds for his leopards, monkeys, bears and rare birds of brilliant plumage.

On the lowest level, hidden from the palace by an avenue of palm trees, lay the barracks, offices, mint, armoury and baths. An aqueduct was constructed to feed the underground cistern, or *aljibe*, with a plentiful supply of fresh water. Architects, engineers and planners were commissioned from Constantinople and Baghdad to complete the work. This was oriental architecture at its best: a harmonious union of edifice, terrace and garden.

The same principles, on a more humble level, apply to the *carmenes*, clustered about the Albaicín hill that overlooks the Alhambra in Granada. The *carmenes* were originally occupied by rich Arab merchants and, like the *cigarrales* of Toledo, were used as country houses. Spectacular views across the rooftops stretch into the distance, the great irrigated *huerta* of grey olive groves and fruit trees falling away beneath the titanic massifs of the Sierra Nevada.

The terraces of the *carmen* are a natural extension of the house: passageways are created by box hedges; small arbours or glorietas are created by the architectural clipping of cypress trees; fragrant borders are formed of lavender and rosemary; and water flows constantly from pools through canals into bubbling fountains. A place to sit out on warm summer evenings, and listen to the rise and fall of the elated cadences of the city.

The earliest surviving garden of Al-Andalus is the Patio of the Orange Trees which extends from the forest of columns in the mosque at Córdoba. It was laid out by the gardeners of Al Mansur in 976, who irrigated the trees with channels fed from three large central fountains. A palm tree, considered sacred by the Arabs, was placed at each corner of the courtyard, to personify reason overcoming fortitude. The only palm groves in Europe are along Spain's southern Mediterranean coast, the most important of which is at Elche near Alicante and was possibly planted by the Phoenicians. In Al-Kahib's *History of Baghdad*, the 'entire height of these trees, from top to bottom was enclosed in carved teak wood, encircled with gilt copper rings.'

Since many of the customs and ways of the Baghdad court were introduced by the minstrel Ziryab, a favourite of Abd al Rahman II, it seems likely that a similar practice occurred in Córdoba. According to Al-Makkari, at the height of the Córdoban caliphate there were over fifty thousand gardens throughout the city, most with a palm tree at their centre.

Another legend, which illustrates the way Al-Andalus was turned into a garden by the Arabs, concerns the poet prince of Seville, Al-Mu'tamid. One day, as he walked along the banks of the river Gua-

Left Some of the most beautiful patios are built about the palaces of Córdoba. Each is christened as are the rooms of the house with an individual name; together they display the best of Moorish garden design and palatial Renaissance architecture.

Right Each *hortus conclusus*, or walled garden, of a palace forms a complete image of paradise in its own right. Purple plumbago reaches to the top of the high dividing walls in the Patio del Pozo (Patio of the Well) in Córdoba.

Above Mosaic pathways formed by black and white river pebbles are a common feature of gardens and courtyards everywhere.

Right Flowers are often individually grown in pots so gardens can appear to be in bloom throughout the year.

Far right Water is often the central feature of a patio and was an indispensable part of garden design. The Moors were great hydraulic technicians and devised ingenious methods of keeping trees and shrubs permanently watered by a series of conduits and channels.

dalquivir, he saw and fell in love with a slave girl called Rumaykiyya. Soon after their marriage he awoke one morning to find his new bride crying as she looked out of the window at snow falling across the sierra. When he asked her what was wrong, Rumaykiyya replied that she was sad because she could not see this beautiful sight every year and wanted to leave immediately for a country where it snowed each winter. Al Mu'tamid, not wishing to offend his wife or be a ruler in exile, ordered his gardeners to plant the hills with almond trees so that in the spring the falling blossoms would create an illusion of snow.

Many similar stories were passed down through the rich poetic traditions of Moorish Spain. The poetry of Al-Andalus was closely linked to the environment. The Arab poets wrote of plains and deserts, of journeys of extraordinary length, of exile and kingdoms in paradisiac lands, of roses, nightingales and love. In their search for an appropriate language to express spiritual meanings, the garden was a frequent muse:

> **T**he dew, the cloud and the scented orchard
> Seemed our tears, our eyelids and your
>   cheek . . .
> (Ibn Hazm, *The Ring of the Dove*, 11th century)

The place where poetry would often have been recited was the interior patio, which was in effect a private garden. For, as Théophile Gautier once remarked, 'the patio is a charming institution', around which the Spanish house is constructed. The writer Georges Sand, spending a winter in the monastery at Valldemosa in Mallorca with her lover Frédéric Chopin, wrote that the patio 'planted with pomegranates, lemons and oranges, surrounded by paved walks, shaded as well . . . by a fragrant arbour, is like a pretty room made of flowers and greenery.'

The patio is an extension of the house, an open-air sitting room ideally suited to hot climates. Since much of day-to-day life happens outside, the patio must be a place for relaxation as well as a thoroughfare for the work of the household. The rooms face on to the patio which gives the occupants a private piece of sky and the simple sense of space calms and soothes the spirit.

The patios of Córdoba, descended from the Roman atrium, are the earliest examples to have survived in Spain. As a prelude to the spring fiesta of Córdoba, there is an annual competition: the patio owners calcimine the walls, often adding a band of coloured wash in a light Moroccan blue to soften the glare. On a walk through the streets surrounding the mosque, it is impossible not to glance through the black *reja* gates leading out into the narrow lanes and make one's own judgements. The typical Córdoban patio is cloistered at ground level, with doors leading into the house from directly beneath the arches. Heavy furniture, chests, chairs and tables are generally placed under the shaded arcades, while ceramics, paintings and flower pots are hung across the walls.

Sevillian patios are generally built to a larger scale, reflecting the prosperity of the city acquired from New World trade, and often contain an upper storey gallery finished with an *artesonado* ceiling. The patios of Granada can either face outwards to the garden, as in the *carmenes*, or inwards facing the interior, when they are normally finished in wood and inlaid or carved in the Mudéjar tradition. Moorish

Right Small brass water jets with moveable nozzles could be directed at flower beds and pathways to dampen the flagstones and create a variety of cooling sounds.

Right Trained vines are the most widespread form of trellising, covering a patio with leafy shade, but wysteria, ivy and bougainvillea also create an effective canopy.

Left Courtyards are often surrounded by colonnades and trellises to create areas of shade at different times of the day.

craftsmen, especially carpenters, remained the predominant influence in Granadan patio design well into the seventeenth century.

Likewise, the monastic cloister is an ecclesiastical interpretation of the patio. Monks and nuns often grew aromatic flowers, especially lilac and roses, in the cloister and other plants for the altar and grave. These cloister-gardens were generally small and modest, but obviously varied according to the architectural style of the age. The Gothic quarter in Barcelona has a series of very remarkable early cloisters where medicinal herbs were grown and distributed to the sick and poor of the city. Catalonia contains, in the early medieval monasteries of Ripoll, San Cugatt and Poblet, three of the most exquisite cloistered gardens known to Europe.

The most famous secular garden of early Christian Spain existed in the Castillo de Olite in Navarre, one of the most magnificent castles of the fifteenth century, built by the Navarrese king Charles the Noble (1387–1425). Charles was particularly fond of horticulture: he ordered his architects to build a large terrace-garden, like the hanging gardens of Babylon, where he grew the orange trees which were eventually introduced into France. He also built a lion's den, and an aviary of wire and iron large enough to contain a pond, some trees and his collection of eagles and falcons.

There was a roof-garden menagerie in the Palaçio de la Almudaina, built for King James II in Palma de Mallorca. It included bears, leopards and monkeys, but the most prized possession of this royal residence was a garden-bathroom complete with hot and cold running water. Water has always been the one essential element of the Spanish garden. Not only is it the central motif and life force of the design, but it is also an effective element of decoration.

Through a series of scoop-wheels, channels, subterranean reservoirs or *aljibes* and artificial lakes, Moorish hydraulic engineers converted areas of Granada, Córdoba, Seville, Murcia and Valencia into vast orchards and *vegas* of citrus groves and silk farms. Water played a central part in Qur'anic rites of ablution, where the washing of hands and feet before prayer was considered essential, and necessitated a constant and plentiful water supply.

Once again, it is the Alhambra which is the most ingenious and vibrant example of Moorish aquatic engineering. Before building began, the waters from the rivers Darro and Genil surrounding the spur on which the palace was built were drawn off by a series of canals from high up near their sources, allowing

209

A*bove* The rich foliage of flowering shrubs carpets almost every available inch of floor and wall in the *carmen*. Plumbago grows particularly well and blooms profusely from September to October.

L*eft* The central fountain in a water garden pond catches the late afternoon light.

enough pressure to feed the fountains, pools and baths. Water was stretched to its full decorative and technical limits so that both its practical and aesthetic qualities could be appreciated to the full. It brims and froths about the edges of the shallow stone channels, running sleekly under dark arches like some long mirror sunk into the marble before gushing up suddenly out of a lotus fountain. It runs through courtyard, chamber, pavilions, gardens, patios and halls joining them into a single, cohesive architectural whole.

Around every corner of the Alhambra, water adopts a different role. In the great Court of the Myrtles it reflects, like a hologram, the interplay of sky and pillared buildings. In the Patio of the Lions it becomes the active centrepiece; from the bubbling central fountain, gracefully supported on the backs of twelve lions representing the twelve months of the year and the twelve signs of the Zodiac, water filters through a series of conduits and small circular pools until it runs into the midst of the slender clusters of white marble columns. In the Partal Gardens, nature takes hold through the pattern of water lilies, the hum of dragonflies and the luxuriant growth of the surrounding shrubs and flowers. Everywhere, water synthesizes the natural with the artificial and is both constant and transitory.

Sitting on the crest of a hill above the Alhambra is the resplendent summer palace known as the Generalife, a word deriving from the Arabic *djannat al-'arif*, meaning 'garden of the architect'. Its position and siting is dramatic; being higher than the Alhambra, it is cooler and therefore greener and ideal for the summer months. Here, water is treated in an even more spectacular way. When the sun starts to sink low in the afternoon sky, the avenue of water sprays that vault over the canal of the inner garden form rainbows in the air. But everywhere the water is gentle; it does not gush or disturb and remains in harmony with the ethereal grace of the buildings and the delicate bloom of the flowers. In the Qur'an paradise is likened to 'a garden full of pavilions running with streams' – through pure decorative understanding, the Alhambra and the Generalife achieve exactly that.

The importance of water is perhaps best expressed by a short Arabic poem engraved about the rim of the lotus fountain in the Patio of the Lions where the substance is likened to a work of art itself:

Running water evokes the illusion of
 being of one substance for the eyes.
Making us ask:

L*eft* Tunnels of climbing plants serve as covered walkways between patios, creating passages of dappled shadow between small outside rooms.

B*elow* Triffid-like agave and ornamental bergenia clamber over the steps of a *carmen*, where the house is approached through the garden.

211

Which is in truth fluid?

Is it the water running over the edge of the
fountain,
Or the monument offering an infinite chan-
nel for the water?

Water plays an even more dramatic role in the
Baroque gardens of La Granja, built beneath the
slopes of the Sierra de Guadarrama. It is only sad
that the fountains consume so much water as to
render them dormant for all but a few afternoons
and evenings of the year. The palace and grounds
are often compared to a French château and there
can be no doubt that the founder, Philip V, was profoundly affected by his upbringing in the nurseries
of Versailles during the reign of Louis XIV. Yet, there
are many details, especially in the treatment of
water, which show how long and deep the oriental
influence ran in Spain. As C. M. Villiers Stuart wrote
when visiting La Granja for the first time in the
1920s:

> **W**hat most struck me was the way the older
> influences had survived the overwhelming
> French invasion. The garden of all others La
> Granja recalled was the Nishat Bagh by the
> Dal lake in Kashmir. The first impression
> may have been due to the long lines of the
> avenues and the dark-blue mountain back-
> ground (alike in both cases), but the charac-
> ter of the ornamental waterfalls, the
> irrigation channels for the trees, and the way
> in which the water from the main canal was
> conducted through the palace, forming a
> fountain in the central dining room, were
> unmistakably Eastern details.
> (From *Spanish Gardens*, 1936)

212

Spain is a land of fountains, and each one is part
of a general manifestation of the Spanish love for
water. In every plaza, cloister, patio and garden there
will be a fountain murmuring, splashing or gushing.
Many are just simple granite basins, but others are
intricately sculpted and decorated with gargoyle
faces from imaginatively carved fonts. Famous spas
exist at Orense, Salamanca, Lanjaron, in the Pyrenees and along the ancient *via de la plata* through
Extremadura: all of them date back to the centuries
of Hispano-Roman rule. Throughout the wildest
sierras *fuentes* still remain by the roadsides, once
used for muleteers but now serving as destinations
for weekend excursions into the countryside. This is
the case even in the north of Spain where water is
plentiful.

A*bove* Yuccas were first introduced to Spain from sub-tropical America. Their stiff lance-like leaves and spikes of gracious white flowers have resulted in the nickname Spanish Bayonet.

L*eft* The central courtyard of this magnificent private palace in Zafra in southern Extremadura is shaded by vast palm trees. The corner fountain is surrounded by simple terracotta flower pots perched on Roman marble column bases.

L*eft* Vast pots of lilies frame the black and white chequered marble floor of the courtyard; green leaves look particularly majestic against patterned *azulejos* dados.

B*elow* Palms held a sacred position in the Moorish courtyard as a symbol of water, the oasis and shaded sanctuary from the desert heat. In Islamic mysticism the palm came to personify reason overcoming trouble.

2**1**3

In more complicated garden decoration a frequent alternative to the fountain was a pavilion or summerhouse, which created privacy and shade from the burning heat of summer. The most fabulous of these, based upon an earlier construction at Hadrian's summer villa at Tivoli, was built by Ma'mun dhu'l-Nun in his eleventh-century palace at Toledo. In the centre of the lake rose a water gazebo of stained glass built around a gold frame. Here the sultan could recline on cushions with his favourites on the hottest day, encircled by the glistening sheath of water falling from the dome. At night candles and torches were lit to illuminate the transparent walls.

Though this palace has since vanished, Toledo possesses some very early gardens, whose first inhabitants were undoubtedly Arabs. Like the *carmenes* of Granada, the *cigarrales* of Toledo were country estates built facing the city, on the far bank of the river Tajo. From there they commanded magnificent views of Spain's ancient Visigothic capital. After the wresting of Toledo from the Arabs in 1085 by Alfonso VI many of these properties were taken over by monastic orders and used as summer retreats in which to escape the heat of Toledo's narrow, sûq-like streets. But with the dissolution of the monasteries in 1836 many of the properties fell into private hands and today they comprise some of the most beautiful country houses in Castile.

Toledo is surrounded by dry, arid and rocky earth, good for little except the regiments of die-hard olive trees filing their way across the surrounding sierras. The gardens of the *cigarrales* are controlled by the harsh extremes of scorching summers and bitterly cold winters. But what is lacking in colour and fertility is made up for by the panoramic view. Prospects radiate out from every avenue and bench, carrying the confines of the garden beyond the ancient almond and olive trees which shape the grounds in front of the house to the distant outline of the city, with its searing Gothic cathedral, *alcázar* and Romanesque brick towers.

The location of the garden was of supreme importance in Islamic garden design. The intention was always to draw the mind and eye first to the horizon, taking in the play of land forms, the curve of the river flowing beneath the steep rockfaces and other significant features. Finally attention rests in the garden itself, where the lines and shapes in the distance were repeated in the foreground with fast-flowing, ornamental water channels, and the sculptural shape of the trees and shrubs. Known as *cigarrales* after the cicadas which chirrup on summer

214

Above The Cigarral de Menores sums up the *cigarral* garden with its far-reaching views of the olive groves beyond and the spires of Toledo in the distance.

Left Plants, such as the coleus, create bright drifts of colour across the ground and have adapted well to both the damp Atlantic climate of the north and the arid earth of the south.

Right Old agricultural terracing below Ronda was originally planted with olives and vines. The land has since been reclaimed and converted into a simple landscaped garden. Tragically the terraces surrounding other less fortunate *pueblos* in Spain have run to seed, the stone walls having collapsed and the top soil eroded.

nights, these estates were bounded by adobe walls, the cracks in their surfaces partially concealed by prickly pear and agave branches. Inside the walls were plantations of mulberry trees for the rearing of silk worms, orchards and gardens planted with apricots, oranges, lemons and fig trees with lilies, geraniums, gilly-flowers and the finest roses in Spain.

The cohesion of the far, middle and immediate distance created a unified impression of a coherent landscaped composition. One of the most illustrious *cigarral*-owners was Gregorio Marañón, doctor, scientific philosopher and historian, who wrote of his home, the Cigarral de Menores, that it was 'the pacifier and restorer of my soul.'

The fame of these early Spanish gardens spread throughout Africa and Asia. Ibn Said, a Moslem born in Granada at the beginning of the thirteenth century, who travelled extensively through the Islamic world, observed: 'The splendour of Andalucia appears to have reached to Tunis, where the sultan is constructing palaces and planting gardens in our manner. All his architects are natives of Andalucia, likewise his gardeners.'

As important as these new forms of garden architecture were the botanical treatises written by Spanish scholars under Islam. The most interesting was a gardening diary written at the height of the Córdoban caliphate by the Mozarabic bishop of Seville, Rabi'ibn Zaid, who had been sent to Syria by Abd al Rahman III to find precious works of art, as well as trees and plants for the palace city of Medina az-Zahra. In his book, he laid down rough guidelines for the seasons, noting their effects upon different crops, and also the weather and astrological expectations for each month, with the reactions to be expected from nature:

> *January* ... The rivers warm; sap rises in the trees; birds pair; Valencian falcons nest and mate; cows deliver calves; ducklings and goslings hatch. This is the month to sow grain and drive in the stakes for the olive, pomegranate and fruit saplings. The first narcissi flower. Trellises are prepared for the vines and other climbing plants; sugar cane is harvested and lemon curd made ...

> *February* ... Birds nest; bees mate and fish begin to stir to the surface of the sea; silkworm eggs are ready to hatch; cranes migrate and saffron bulbs and spring cabbage sown; fruit trees should be grafted, especially apples and pears; letters should be sent out to recruit summer workers; the first

Views across the old city wall of Ronda. Neatly clipped box hedges and topiary lend an air of formality.

Right Prospects and location are indispensible ingredients for the Spanish garden. Carefully planned vistas control the sense of space, preventing it from becoming overpowering.

Left Stucco walls are sometimes painted a butter ochre, creating a strong contrast with the green foliage.

Right Fountains, walls and pebbled mosaics are three ways of drawing the attention of mind and eye away from the distance.

swallows return to their nests; truffles and wild asparagus can be found in the forests and meadows . . .

March . . . Fig trees are grafted; shoots appear; Valencian hawks lay eggs; sugar beet is planted; lilies begin to flower; silkworms hatch; garden beans ripen; sturgeon swim into the rivers; cucumbers, cotton, crocus, eggplants, marjoram and mint are sown; locusts swarm and should be killed at the first opportunity without hesitation.
(*The Calendar of Córdoba in the year* 961, quoted from *Moorish Culture in Spain*, Titus Burckhardt, trans. Alisa Jaffa, 1972)

From these brief excerpts from just three months it is interesting to note the variety and number of crops. Every flower known to Europe grows in the climate of Spain, as well as most from sub-tropical climates. There is no month of the year without its bloom; and of course there was a close link between physical health and the garden.

Through the translation of Greek texts the Arabs were able to investigate the particular medicinal qualities possessed by each fruit, flower and herb. In line with Pliny's *Natural History*, they believed that human illness occurred when the elemental equilibrium of the body was upset, and that every plant had its particular curative powers. A succession of Arab pharmacognosists researched these properties among them the Malagueño, Ibn Baytar, who listed over 1,400 medicines, many of which he discovered himself.

The botanical tradition has been strong in Spain ever since the twelfth century, when a Sevillian farmer, Abu Zacaria Amed Ibn al-Awwan, wrote a book on agriculture with two of its chapters devoted to ornamental shrubs, herbs, flowers and trees with planting tips for the gardener. It remained the agrarian bible until well after the Christian reconquest and the final expulsion of the Moors in 1610. The first botanical garden on the continent was established in the fourteenth century at Guadix, on the borders of the kingdom of Granada, in the palace grounds of King Naser. It was tended by a herbal doctor, Mohammed Ben Alí Ben Pharah, known as Alschaphra, and included plants from India, Persia and Syria.

However, with the discovery of the Americas, the study of botany was transformed and whole new horizons opened up for research. One of the reasons which eventually persuaded Queen Isabella of Castile to finance the first voyage of Christopher Colum-

218

bus was the future admiral's deep understanding of nature. Before setting out west, Columbus had travelled to Chios to watch the mastic harvest; and on other occasions he had visited Guinea, Madeira, Sardinia and Sicily, where he had carefully logged information about their insular flora and fauna, their climate and seasonal changes. In a memorandum on his second voyage, he noted the progress of the garden planted by a garrison left at Hispaniola:

> We are quite certain, as the progress shows, that in this land both wheat and wine will easily be produced; but we must wait for the fruit and flowers and sugar cane before being absolutely sure the land is as fertile as the earth of Andalucia and Sicily.

Hernán Cortés reported on the luxurious gardens of the Aztec kings. But it was Philip II's doctor, Andrés Laguna, who above all helped to promote early exploration into the botany of the Americas. As a young adviser to Pope Julius III in Rome, he had personally witnessed the establishment of the first two botanical gardens in Italy at Padua and Pisa, and was inspired to translate into Spanish a treatise on botany written by the Greek scholar, Dioscorides. After returning to Spain, he persuaded Philip II to establish a botanical garden at the new royal palace at Aranjuez, and to finance an expedition to New Spain in Mexico with the sole purpose of returning with rare and previously unrecorded plant and tree specimens.

The results of this journey, which eventually took place between 1571 and 1577 after Laguna's death, were recorded in a sixteen-volume work written by the head of the expedition, Francisco Hernández. Unfortunately the only original copy of this great work was destroyed by a fire in the library at El Escorial in 1671 and the ten volumes of illustrations were lost forever, but a copy of the manuscript miraculously turned up in the eighteenth century and from it can be gathered the immense importance of the expedition. Hernández spent a great deal of time recording details of Aztec medicines and the practises of the Indian herbalists, which were later adopted by the pharmacies of Spain. His knowledge helped to promote such interest that small private botanical gardens were established in Seville, Cadiz, Valencia and the Canary Islands, where the tropical climate was particularly favourable to many of these plants.

The gardens of the Habsburg kings were understandably conceived on a majesterial scale. In the Austrian palaces surrounding Madrid, in the Casa

Far left A grand avenue of lush palm trees. Spain possesses the only palm groves in Europe. The oldest, at Elche near Alicante, was possibly planted by Phoenician settlers.

Left Large amphorae and *tinajas*, once used for carrying and storing olives, wine and oil, now serve as flower pots in private gardens and patios everywhere.

Below A small water pavilion on a lake in the Maria Luisa Park is a romantic Neo-Arabic touch added by J. Forestier, who designed the gardens for the Ibero-American Exhibition of 1929.

219

Right La Granja was built by Philip V, the first Bourbon king of Spain, who had been educated at the court at Versailles. He used the palace as his summer residence before retiring there after his abdication. He is buried beside his wife Isabella Farnese in a tomb in the chapel.

Far right above The parterres and great woodland of chestnuts and elms covers an area of 360 acres, criss-crossed by pathways stretching for over twenty miles. The garden was originally laid out by René Carlier, and was continued after his death by Etienne Boutelou, the head gardener at Aranjuez.

Far right below The twenty-six main fountains of La Granja, near Segovia, are even more outrageous than those of Versailles. They are based upon themes from classical mythology and are set within magnificent gardens, rising gently up a slope beneath the Sierra de Guadarrama.

de Campo, Palacio del Pardo and the hunting estates near El Escorial, the Flemish-inspired gardens were designed on a scale which the later Bourbon monarchs, under the heavy influence of Versailles, could not match for splendour and extravagance. Sadly, only remnants of the original ground plans have remained.

The royal palace at Aranjuez was undoubtedly the most ambitious of these projects begun by Philip II's architect, Juan de Herrera, and his head gardener, Jerónimo Algora. The original plans for the garden included grounds for the huge royal palace, a complete village, an extensive arboretum and an island garden of fountains and classical statues built about a right-angled bend in the river Tajo and joined by a long canal. There exists a strange fantastical drawing of a vast trellised avenue, where people walking in the shade of the climbing roses growing over the gargantuan metal structure are the size of ants crawling about a Gothic cathedral. Unfortunately it was one more plan never realized and the gardens and palaces open to the public today are of a much later date.

There are few original Renaissance gardens in Spain. El Bosque in the isolated town of Béjar in the province of Avila has run completely to seed but in

221

Far right The Pazo de Oca was once completely self-sufficient and produced its own fruit, vegetables and wheat, wove linen from the estate flax and fermented wine from grapes grown on tall pergolas – a common farming practice in Galicia.

Right A different interpretation of the Baroque garden developed in Galicia during the eighteenth century around the farm estates known as *pazos*. At the Pazo de Oca, the upper pond, with a granite boat covered in hydrangeas and manned by a master and his servant, represents the tranquil waters of heaven.

the large granite ponds and small ruined pavilions something of the dignity of the age can be imagined. Only in the garden-courtyards of the Renaissance urban palaces, often resembling the *giardino secreto* of the Italians and those gardens so delicately depicted in Flemish painting, has something of the authentic feeling of the age been preserved.

The most magnificent testament to the courtly extravagance of the seventeenth century were the gardens inaugurated by Philip IV's chief minister, the Conde-Duque Olivares. He commissioned the Italian garden architect Cosme Lotti, who had worked on the Boboli gardens of the Palazzo Pitti in Florence, to surround the sumptuous palace of Buen Retiro, situated on a hillside overlooking Madrid, with grounds suitable to the temperament and fashions of the time. Even today, the Buen Retiro Park, like a green island rising from the sprawl of the busy capital, retains its air of theatricality and bursts with excitement every Saturday and Sunday when the main *paseo* throngs with life: tarot card readers, chiromancers, marionettes, puppetteers, gypsies selling medicinal twigs, buskers, saxophonists, steel bands, clowns and pavement artists.

What Lotti produced for the court of Philip IV was very different. The park was an open air theatre for

the nobility with a lionhouse, an arena for bullfights, an outside ballroom and space to accommodate the aviary of Olivares, filled with birds captured in the New World. The centrepiece was a vast lake on the waters of which were enacted simulated naval battles, or *naumaquias*, and water-borne operas written by the great court playwright of the age, Pedro Calderón de la Barca.

One of the most spectacular of these productions took place in 1635. Entitled *The Spell of Circe*, it was an allegory on the seduction of Ulysses by a sorceress. A small floating island was built in the middle of the lake and the whole set illuminated by thousands of wax torches and candles hanging in the trees, by bonfires and firecrackers, exploding volcanoes and other special effects. The spectacle culminated in the apparition of Circe riding across the water in a chariot pulled by dolphins.

The Retiro was undoubtedly planted with many strange trees and shrubs discovered in the newly conquered territories on the far side of the Atlantic, but it was not until the eighteenth century that purely botanical explorations set sail. During the reign of Charles III, expeditions penetrated into equatorial America, into Brazil, Chile, Peru, Colombia, over the Andes, through the Amazon basin, into

223

the Philippines and across many islands in the Pacific Ocean. The most important discovery was undoubtedly the Chinchona tree, whose alkaline bark produced quinine, the only known treatment for malaria. New plants such as the fuchsia and gardenia became popular in the gardens of Europe.

The most representative type of garden in this botanical age of discovery was the Galician *pazo* – a shortening of the word *palacio*. Many of these garden-farm estates date back to Roman times, but it was in the seventeenth and eighteenth centuries that they acquired their present identities. At this time there were close religious and governmental ties between the north-western corner of Spain and the Americas. Santiago de Compostela afforded an extensive botanical garden and arboretum, dedicated to the flora of Argentina.

The dominant characteristic of the Galician *pazo* is the exuberant virescence of the vegetation. Rhododendrons, camellias, azaleas and Chinese magnolia trees often grow so vigorously as to appear subtropical. The ornamentation in the garden is almost entirely sculpted from the heavy, grey local granite and the imagery spans the religious, figurative, ancestral and geometric. Once again, water is used to connect the house and garden with the enveloping landscape. The Marquesa de Casa Valdés, who was brought up in a *pazo* and later in life wrote the classic history of Spanish gardens, described a *pazo* as follows:

> The gardens of Galicia, however strange it may sound, are gardens of winter, best visited in the clouds and mists. That is when they become scenes of extraordinary flowering, true explosions of colour. In February the camellias and mimosas start to bloom, and in the mild Atlantic climate these trees, which remain mere shrubs in other countries, acquire exalted proportions. During the winter these gardens shine with pure, unblemished white camellias and red camelias with a relucent intensity. The pazos of Galicia are extraordinarily beautiful and it is impossible to speak of them without sounding nostalgic.
> (*Jardines de España*, first published 1950)

This nostalgia lives on through the melancholic growth of moss across the stone and tree trunks; through the simple, pastoral expressions of the statues, dressed in local Galician costumes with faces

25

Far *left* Water is plentiful in northern gardens in contrast to the south of Spain where it is scarce. Rushing through channels and splashing over fountains with playful extravagance, it forms a link between house, garden and estate.

Left In a climate of mist and rain where water is abundant, plants, shrubs and trees grow to tropical proportions. In late winter the camellias, mimosas, rhododendrons and azaleas burst into bloom and the garden looks its most impressive. Here, amaryllis lilies flourish at the foot of a sunny south-facing wall, submerged under a thick covering of Viriginia creeper.

Above Lichen and moss dress every inch of granite which is the other distinguishing feature of the *pazo* garden. At Oca, the unyielding stone has been boldly hewn into spheres, bridges and battlements which accentuate the perspective along the long tree-and shrub-lined avenues.

Left Apart from water, the simple sculptural qualities of pots and plants mingled with explosions of pure colour are the two characteristics linking the dry- and wet-climate gardens.

Right In Castile, the silvery-green shades of the olive leaf, the aroma released by carpets of lavender into the strong winds of late autumn and the still silence of summer combine to create the simplest but most natural form of garden in Spain.

226 weathered by the incessant showers of rain; and in the semi-fortified façades of the manor houses, reminiscent of the conflicts of Galician nobility.

While Galicia explored its own form of Baroque, the rest of Spanish garden design derived its influence from the Neo-classic. The new Bourbon palace at Aranjuez, the Retiro Park and gardens of El Escorial were remodelled along French and Italian lines with parterres, plenty of classically inspired sculpture, topiary and box hedging, and folly-like pavilions. The creation of the gardens at Horta in Barcelona and Monforte in Valencia towards the end of the eighteenth century typified this Europeanization of taste. However, with the dawning of the nineteenth century all this disappeared, as the penchant for lakes, grottoes and artificial mountains spread through public parks and gardens; conserva-

tories became a common feature of houses, especially in northern resorts.

By the end of the century, the spirit of originality which had established itself in architecture and industrial design began to influence the form of the Spanish garden. A period of Neo-Arabism was inaugurated by the French landscape designer J. Forestier, who designed the Maria Luisa Park for the 1929 Ibero-American Exhibition. He adopted the materials common to the Moorish garden – bricks, tiles and whitewash – and created avenues lined with magnolias, palms, chestnuts, pecans, even banana trees. Open spaces were embellished with marble statues of local writers and poets. He was also responsible for the design of many private gardens all over the country, but he is perhaps most curiously remembered for the house and garden he

created in the last years of his life in the Bois de Boulogne in Paris, which was later lived in by the Duke and Duchess of Windsor.

The combination of sharp climatic variations, improved horticultural methods and the influx of north European enthusiasm, has undoubtedly contributed to a resurgence of interest in gardens in the last few decades. The ancient Arab gardens of Al-Andalus continue to represent the perfect alliance of oriental taste in an occidental setting. It is not surprising that they are still an inspiration to gardeners throughout the world. Of a different nature are the near tropical gardens of the north, and the dry, evergreen gardens of Castile which, through their subtle hues and their struggle with a harsh, unyielding environment, present a more deeply Spanish interpretation of paradise.

MODERNISM

By reinterpreting

the architecture of the past

and adopting the new industrial formulas of the nineteenth century,

the Modernismo movement developed an artistic vision that operated on many levels.

It became more than a flamboyant aesthetic style,

bearing important implications

for Catalan nationalism

and the cultural

Renaissance.

In 1854 the old walls of Barcelona were knocked down to make room for an expanding, successful city. Dreams of industrial wealth were beginning to drain the provinces of people, many of them ruined by the Carlist wars and the unsettled rural economy. The loss of the Spanish colonies brought families back from the Americas to begin new lives in Spain. With this increased activity Catalonia, in particular, began to change and life was re-evaluated on every front. The general discontent was blamed on centralized government and a political system conducted, so Catalans thought, by a corrupt and insensitive bureaucracy in Madrid. Why should their dynamism and economic success be used to support and maintain an outdated and stultified government? From this new, outspoken confidence a cultural renaissance emerged.

The Catalan *renaixença* began in the 1830s with a revived interest in the Catalan language, which had lain dormant for centuries except in a few isolated villages. It rapidly became the adopted tongue of poets and writers, and then spread into everyday speech. Catalans sought to recover the cultural splendour of that Golden Age when the Aragónese-Catalan kingdom ruled over a Mediterranean empire. This aim found a voice in the first Catalan

230

Far *left above* As people began to migrate from the provinces into the big cities complete new neighbourhoods, like the Eixample in Barcelona, were constructed. Mass production of tiles presented a cheap means of decorating the façades of plain buildings with bright colour and pattern.

Left *above* Enlarged populations demanded convenient shopping facilities and vast cathedral-sized markets were erected in the centre of these new prosperous suburbs, often constructed with naked girders and stained glass.

Left *below* Artists of the Modernismo movement adopted a naturalistic approach to design using plants, water lilies and leaves as the basis for arabesque patterns.

Right The most theatrical decoration was reserved for architectural façades, where the Spanish love of ornament and flamboyance, which had lain dormant since the Baroque age, came to the fore. The whole façade of this house in Barcelona is covered in sea-green ceramic tiles, its windows framed with plaster decoration moulded into sweeping shapes that billow like waves.

231

L*eft* What architects searched for was the *obra total*, the total work, where all art forms including ironwork, carpentry, masonry and furniture design merged to create a building which might be considered as a work of art in itself as well as a piece of practical architecture.

R*ight* The chimneys on the roof of Gaudí's Casa Milà became pieces of sculpture in their own right and were shaped to look like African tribal masks and the helmeted heads of medieval knights.

Above One of Gaudí's earliest commissions was the Casa El Capricho in the summer resort town of Comillas. The exterior was heavily ornamented with ceramic sunflowers and coloured bricks to coordinate with the natural green of the grass and the golden sand of the coast.

Right Gothic, Arabic and Islamic details were effectively combined in Gaudí's work, while strong religious imagery frequently appeared.

Left Façades of buildings were treated with equal originality. In the Casa Batlló, designed by Gaudí, supporting pillars were shaped like tyrannosauric bones, balconies stared across the street like Venetian carnival masks and roof tiles were glazed and shaped to simulate the scales of a dragon.

newspaper, the D*iari Català*, established in 1881. The essential message was plain: regional autonomy for the Catalans.

The financial impetus for this movement was supplied by a burgeoning group of rich industrialists who were prepared to sponsor artists and employ new ideas and designs in their plans for expansion. Their example inspired every level of cultivated Catalan society. In 1888 the city government sponsored a Universal Exhibition which, for the first time, expounded this new *catalanismo*. It created an international image for the city, as well as having the important psychological effect of defining Catalan style to its own people.

This revival had repercussions on every one of the arts, but the greatest innovations were in architecture, where the new industrial methods could be explored in depth. In 1878 the architect and public figure, Lluis Domènech i Mortamer, wrote that for *catalanismo* to discover itself, it must search for a national architecture. His words took on greater significance in the light of the theories of the French architect Viollet-le-Duc, the reviver of medieval architecture. He had declared that the responsibility of the architect was to uncover the history of national architecture and reinterpret it in a contemporary context. The movement which derives from these ideas was known in Spain as Modernismo.

In its early stages Modernism was an eclectic movement which assimilated numerous fashions and ideas from the rest of Europe. The esoteric passion for romantic medievalism, which characterized the English Pre-Raphaelite movement, was one such influence. But it soon found its own identity in the work of three major architects: Lluis Domènech i Mortamer, Josep Puig i Cadafalch and, most brilliant of them all, Antoni Gaudí i Cornet. These figures are generally credited with inspiring the movement, but at least fifty other architects and craftsmen were directly involved, as well as numerous painters, sculptors and smiths. The new ideas spread into all areas of industrial design, into printing, jewellery, furniture and also civic design, as seen in benches, street lamps and railings.

The Modernismo movement had a relatively short life span from 1880 to 1916, and was the Spanish response to such contemporary European movements as Art Nouveau in France, Stile Liberta in Italy and Jugendstil in Germany.

John Ruskin's view that 'ornament is the origin of architecture' made an undoubted impression upon the attitudes of the age. The Modernists adopted a naturalistic approach to art using plants, water lilies

235

and leaves as the basis of much design, exaggerated by the Spanish love of ornament and flamboyance, which had lain dormant since the Baroque age. New techniques were used to create an effect, such as the attachment of cast iron elements to solid or laminated masonry, and new materials such as sheet iron, industrial glass and reinforced concrete were extensively used. Columns were cast to look like tyrannosauric bones. Roof tiles became the scales of imaginary monsters. Balconies became grotesque mouths, while snails and crocodiles crawled up façades.

Modernist symbolism on another level was profoundly Gothic. Catalonia was steeped in the Gothic tradition, the architecture of its medieval empire. The hall-churches and cathedrals of Palma de Mallorca, Gerona and Barcelona were the architectural testament of former greatness. A return to this form was a way of escaping the full, authoritarian Classicism which had been imposed upon Spain ever since the reign of Charles III. Neo-Gothic became the architecture of this new expressionism, and in its elevated form and flamboyant decoration was intended, above all, to inspire.

So merlons, shields, angels and gargoyles were once again perched on the corners and façades of

Far left The undulating front of the Casa Milà in the new Eixample district of Barcelona was Gaudí's masterpiece of urban architecture.

Left This entrance hall and staircase is possessed of strong organic undercurrents to which the articulation of structure is sacrificed in Modernist buildings.

Right The Baroque love of curves and architectonic features, like this upper storey loggia, was exuberantly reinterpreted with large doses of almost fairytale fantasy.

237

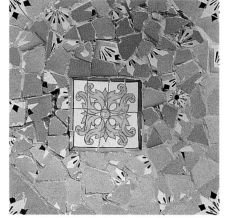

new buildings; narrow windows with pointed arches were used in the design of apartment blocks; even electric light bulbs, gramophones, telephones and cameras became vehicles for 'new age' decoration. Everyday life responded to the symbolism of the Catalan *renaixença*.

The Islamic tradition of Spain, too, was reinterpreted and freely adapted within the Modernist framework. The use of exposed laminated brick and rubblestone is a common feature of many Modernist buildings just as the use of tiles and ceramics was liberally adopted as a cheap means of giving life and colour to architecture. The ceramic factory at Ramises flourished as complete façades and interiors were covered with tiles. Much of this innovative work was done by J. Jujol, a close associate of Gaudí's, who used appliqués and irregularly-shaped pieces of glazed tile and glass to create abstract patterns. Gaudí's Palacio Güell was based upon the Islamic design of the Alhambra. In 1874 he made a journey to North Africa with the Marqués de Comillas specifically to examine the architecture of Morocco and the Arabic influence on Mudéjar style. Soon afterwards he designed a Spanish Franciscan mission school in Tangier: it was never realized, but the plans were later incorporated into the cathedral of the Sagrada Familia.

Gaudí once claimed that the straight line belonged to man but the curved line to God. The Modernist attitude to line considered and tested almost every conceivable option between the two: parabolic arches, helicoidal chimneys, acute and obtuse angles, leaning pillars, fluid arching columns and jostling geometrics. The Eixample, the new area of Barcelona where many of the most important Modernist buildings can still be admired, was laid out by Ildefons Cerdá from 1860 onwards. It is an example of logical urban planning where the streets run at right angles to each other and parallel to the sea, where boulevards are wide and planted with trees – an ideal environment created for the new cultivated classes. The Modernist buildings, especially those built along the Passeig de Gràcia, are in complete contrast to these ordered symmetries. The undulating lines and innovative shapes give a certain movement to the street, with façades that emulate cliffs, waves and rockfaces.

The treatment of interiors was equally important. In the search for coherent aesthetic coordination between the outside and inside, Gaudí worked with major artisans of the time. What Modernist architects were searching for was the *obra total* – the 'total work', the harnessing of all industrial technology to

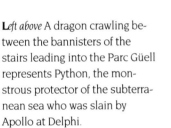

Left above A dragon crawling between the bannisters of the stairs leading into the Parc Güell represents Python, the monstrous protector of the subterranean sea who was slain by Apollo at Delphi.

Left below Glistening collages of rejected ceramic chips and *faïence* fragments were pressed into the wet mortar covering the surfaces of thousands of square feet of the park. Gaudí collaborated with the ceramicist J. M. Jujol in all these sumptuous designs, including the serpentine bench overlooking the city.

Right As far as possible Gaudí tried to leave the natural contours of the park as he found them, and devised several shaded passageways where the supporting structure followed the natural gradient of the slope.

239

The Sociedad General de Autores (Society of Authors) is one of the few Modernist buildings in Madrid that remain intact. The main staircase is an outstanding example of an interior *obra total* where iron, marble, bronze and glass have been welded together into a wild, florid design.

A*bove* The glowing stained-glass cupola above the main foyer of the Palace Hotel, built between 1913 and 1914, combined fresh industrial colours with simple Art Nouveau motifs. It became an important meeting place for progressive Madrilènos.

241

R*ight* Stained glass was extensively used for interiors and effectively diffused the strong Iberian light. Furniture designs, even floorboards, were invested with an equal eye to originality.

A*bove and right* The courtyard of the Casa Macaya is one of the most accomplished works by Josep Puig i Cadafalch, whose style was inspired by Gothic elements. In the delicate painted borders and wainscots, and the stained glass *ajimez* windows, he captured the essence of Neo-Gothic sentiment.

L*eft* Catalonia's period of medieval Gothic splendour ran deep through Modernist thought. Gothic architecture was considered expressive and uplifting while the long period of imposed Classicism seemed dehumanized and academic.

Left Large iron gates, shaped like a colossal spider's web, create an entrance and exit for pedestrians and cars into the Casa Milà. Gaudí once claimed that the straight line belonged to man but the curved line belonged to God.

Right above Wrought-iron has been worked with as much delicacy as the ornate masonry surrounding this Modernist fireplace. The overall impression, even with the built-in clock, is of a monstrous face.

Right below A simple exterior gate resembles the wings of a butterfly and at once possesses grace and delicacy as well as a sense of impenetrability. Though Modernismo often appears a whimsical style it never ceased to perform basic functional tasks.

an aesthetic end, a sculptural metaphor brought to life through colour and line.

The movement soon spread throughout Catalonia, where other cities were undergoing spectacular growth as the railway opened up new areas to development. Gerona, coastal resort towns like Sitges and even the monastery of Montserrat, the spiritual heart of *catalanismo*, all were touched by the new architectural idealism. While new social attitudes were expressed through the construction of housing estates for factory workers, mills, markets, industrial compounds, cooperative *bodegas* and schools put it into practical form. It was all part of the vision of a new society.

No single figure captured and interpreted the architectural innovations of Modernismo as well as Antoni Gaudí. He was born into a humble family in Reus, near Tarragona, in 1852 and attributed a great deal to his ancestral background. Later in life, when asked about the sculptural elements of his architecture, he commented:

> I possess a spatial understanding because I am the son, grandson and great-grandson of coppersmiths. On my mother's side of the family there were also smiths, coopers and sailors who each understood space and matter. The smith is a man who can make shape from a sheet, while the metalsmith understands all three dimensions and thus unconsciously achieves a dominion over space which not everybody possesses.

At the age of fifteen, Gaudí designed a project for the restoration of the abandoned Cistercian monastery of Poblet, and his early drawings at university showed a tendency towards Romantic classicism and the Neo-Baroque. In 1878 he qualified as an architect and entered the mainstream of Barcelona's artistic community, mixing with people who would later become established figures of the new movement. His early commissions included designs for the interior of a pharmacy; statues in the lake of the Parque de Ciudadela, built for the Exposition of 1888; and streetlamps and a new lighting system for the waterfront.

Gaudí's life was to change radically as a consequence of his meeting with Eusebi Güell, a rich textile manufacturer who was to become the most active exponent of Gaudí's architectural vision. Güell, like Gaudí, was an ardent supporter of the New Catalonia and their relationship produced a profound change in the young architect's attitudes. Gaudí refused to speak any language other than

Catalan to his workers, and even the king. Towards the end of the century his work began to take on a more organic maturity, and each of his commissions after 1900 show an individuality in which architectural form echoes, if not exaggerates, its underlying structure.

As part of his plans for the Güell estate, Gaudí proposed a colony of about sixty houses on a hill on the north-west side of Barcelona, overlooking the city. It was to be surrounded by a landscaped garden in the English manner, where the architecture would fuse naturally with the terrain. Only the garden and two houses were ever built; and in 1922 the site was bought by the city council and turned into a municipal park. But in the cavernous passageways, leaning at an angle with the slope of the hillsides, and in the undulating line of the perimeter wall that follows the lie of the land, the organic emphasis of Gaudí's work can be clearly appreciated. The vast serpentine bench, decorated with *trencadís*, or broken ceramic piece, is as much a work of sculpture as a practical

piece of urban design.

Gaudí then embarked on the building of two of his most accomplished civic buildings, both of which are to be found in the Passeig de Gràcia. The Casa Batlló, with its elephantine feet planted firmly on the pavement, is a profusion of forms and motifs, stained glass windows, a first-floor loggia and a fantastic ceramic-tiled roof that resembles the back of a dragon. The interior contains some of Gaudí's most accomplished furniture designs, including a magnificent wooden fireplace and many glass and wrought-iron elements. The structure of the Casa Milá was even more audacious, with a façade that looked like the soft undulations of sand left by the receding tide and a roof of chimneys shaped like medieval helmets.

But it was the Sagrada Familia which occupied the architect's imagination obsessively from 1916 onwards, when Gaudí developed a deeply religious vocation. There is no building like it in the history of architecture. Gaudí referred to it as his 'mystic hive' and though over a hundred years have passed since construction work on the cathedral first began, only a fraction has been completed. The main source of inspiration is Gothic, but Gaudí was constantly revising his plans with his distinctive freehand drawings. The final project was to consist of eighteen towers: twelve to represent each of the apostles, four more for the evangelists, another for the Virgin, while the largest would soar to a height of over five hundred feet as a symbol of the life of Christ. Each window and column would represent the work of a saint or a familiar scene from the bible.

After 1918 taste turned against Modernism and there was a return to a more classical style in a movement known as *noucentism*. Nevertheless, the confidence and energy of the Modernismo movement lived on through the work of artists such as González, Picasso, Miró and Dalí. In its strange interpretation of line and form Modernismo had an elemental influence on the art of every generation of the twentieth century.

246

Left The influence of Modernismo travelled throughout Catalan Spain. No industrial art remained unaffected as buildings down to the last details on door frames fell beneath the movement's spell.

Left The Sagrada Familia, Gaudí's unfinished *magnum opus*, crawls with the zealously religious symbolism of its creator, who never ceased to be inspired by the enigmas of nature. Gaudí imagined his 'mystic hive' to be the architectural embodiment of the life of Christ.

Right Gaudí spent the last years of his life sleeping in a hut beside the cathedral and devoting all his time to its completion. Following his death in a road accident in 1926, work has been sporadic and the greater part of his architectural vision remains unrealized. But the Sagrada Familia stands as a symbol of the genius of Gaudí and the Modernismo movement.

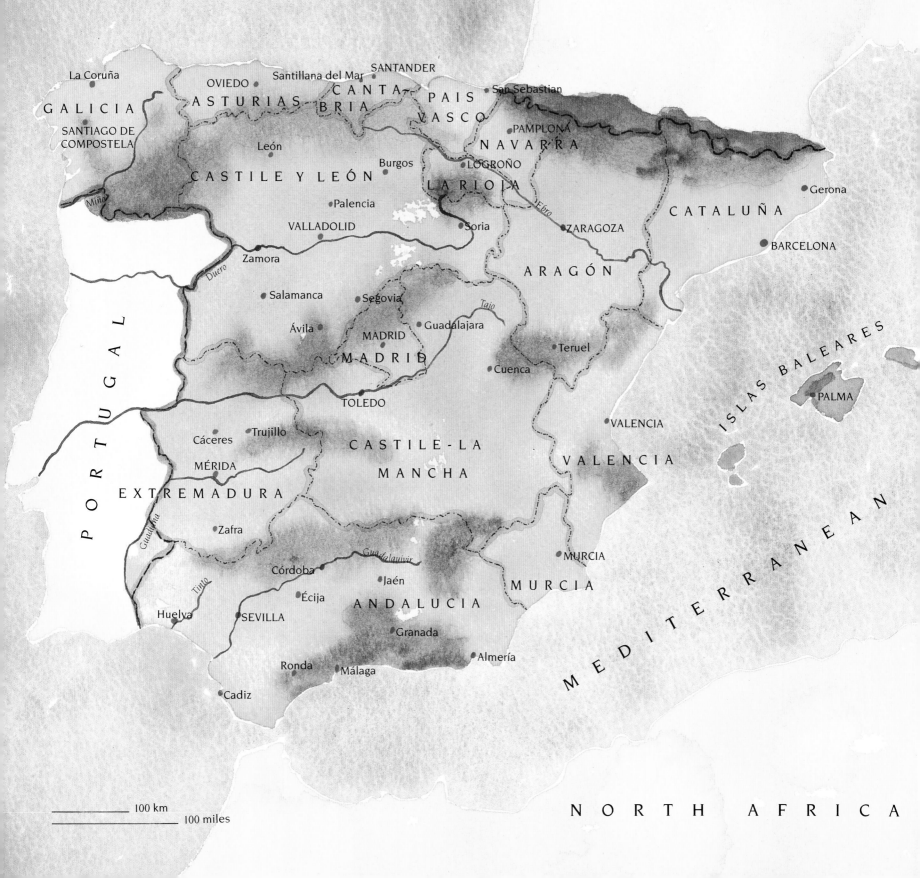

ATLANTIC

FRANCE

La Coruña

GALICIA

SANTIAGO DE
COMPOSTELA

Miño

P
O
R
T
U
G
A
L

OVIEDO

ASTURIAS

León

CASTILE Y LEÓN

Palencia

VALLADOLID

Zamora

Duero

Salamanca

Ávila

Santillana del Mar   SANTANDER

CANTA-
BRIA

PAIS
VASCO

San Sebastian

PAMPLONA

NAVARRA

Burgos

Soria

Segovia

Guadalajara

MADRID

MADRID

Tajo

LOGROÑO

LA RIOJA

Ebro

ZARAGOZA

ARAGÓN

Teruel

Cuenca

Gerona

CATALUÑA

BARCELONA

ISLAS
BALEARES

Cáceres   Trujillo

MÉRIDA

EXTREMADURA

Guadiana

Zafra

Tinto

Huelva

SEVILLA

Cadiz

Córdoba

Écija

Ronda

Málaga

TOLEDO

CASTILE-LA
MANCHA

Guadalquivir

Jaén

ANDALUCIA

Granada

VALENCIA

VALENCIA

MURCIA

MURCIA

Almería

PALMA

M
E
D
I
T
E
R
R
A
N
E
A
N

100 km

100 miles

NORTH   AFRICA

The map of Spain on p. 248 gives the authentic Spanish place names. Where such names have become common usage in a slightly different form, these have been used throughout in the text. For example, Sevilla is referred to as Seville, Cataluña as Catalonia, Navarra as Navarre and Pais Vasco as the Basque Country.

GLOSSARY

Adobe Mud and wattle from which sun-dried building bricks are made.

Ajimez A twin-light window, its coupled arches divided by a central column.

Alcázar Castle, fortress or citadel.

Alegría Happiness, joy.

Aljibe Subterranean reservoir or cistern.

Amorini Cherub.

Artesonado Coffered ceiling of polychromed or inlaid wood derived from Mudéjar marquetry.

Azulejo Glazed, ornamental tile.

Bargueño Chest with drawers, normally highly decorated.

Bodega Wine cellar.

Caballero Rider, horseman.

Cañadas Transhumant sheep trail.

Carmen Country house or villa; collective term for houses on the Albaicìn hill opposite the Alhambra in Granada.

Castellano The Castilian language; or a general term for Spanish.

Castillo Castle.

Chahar bagh Persian garden, typically quartered by four water channels.

Churrigueresque Exhuberantly ornamental variant of Baroque style named after the eighteenth-century architect, José Churriguera.

Cigarral Country house; collective term for villas overlooking Toledo.

Cortijo Andalucian farm house.

Dehesa Wild plains of meadowland with cork and oak used as grazing pasture in Extremadura.

Escudo Coat-of-arms.

Esgrafiado Decorative finish given to exterior walls.

Esparto Woven grass matting.

Fuente Fountain, spring.

Huerta Kitchen gardens and allotments surrounding many rural villages.

Lacerías Delicate lace-like stucco carving.

Meseta The central tableland comprising much of mainland Spain.

Mezquita The great mosque of Córdoba.

Mozarabic Term for Christian art produced under the influence of Arab rule.

Mudéjar Term for Arab art produced under the influence of Christian rule.

Naumaquias Water operas, particularly popular in late Habsburg courts.

Paseo Promenade.

Pasos Group of carved figures carried in religious procession.

Pintor de Imaginería Painter employed by the church to refurbish the polychrome work in church interiors.

Plateresque Late Gothic-early Renaissance style of architecture with intricate decoration which resembles the work of silversmiths (*platerías*).

Pueblo Town or village and the community of people who live in it.

Reconquista Historical term applied to the gradual reconquest of land by the Christians from the Arabs.

Reja Wrought-iron screen protecting side altars in a church or cathedral.

Renaixença Nineteenth-century cultural renaissance in Catalonia which included the Modernismo movement.

Retablo Retable; ornamental screen above an altar.

Rías Deep river fjords of Galicia.

Serranía Mountain range.

Son Collective term applied to the country farm estates of Mallorca.

Talayots Megalithic monuments in the Balearic Islands, possibly used as sacrificial or funerary altars.

Taracea Marquetry.

Tinaja Earthenware storage vats.

Tertulia Literary or artistic gathering.

Vega Irrigated land, fertile plain.

Verja An altar surround of decorative ironwork.

INDEX

ACKNOWLEDGEMENTS

Maloli Castro

María Cabanyes

Mónica Luengo

Maria Medina

Mayte Goizueta

Belen López de Diego

Gregorio Marañon

Gerard Quirk

Agustin Barrenechea-Arando Cataliá

Ultramar Express Espagna

James H. Ward

Rafael Blázquez Godoy

Jaime Arias

Fernando Chueca

Rafael Manzano

Paco Peris

Carlos Sanchez

Juan Pol

Enrique Pérez Torres

Ignacio Medina, Duque de Segorbe

Antonio Lobato

Denny Hemming

Jeremy Catto

We would like to thank the Professional Photography Division
of the **Eastman Kodak Company** for their contribution to this book.

The Kodak films used by Amparo Garrido whilst on location for **SPAIN** are as follows:
For landscapes and exteriors
Ektachrome 64
Professional EPR

For interiors with natural light
Ektachrome 100
Professional EPN

For interiors with artificial light
Ektachrome 160
Professional EPT

AVIS *RENT A CAR*

We would like to thank **Avis Rent a Car** for their contribution to this book.

We would like to thank **Iberia Airlines** for their contribution to this book.